THE HOUSE OF
GWYNNE

THE HOUSE OF
GWYNNE

CARS, PUMPS & AEROENGINES
1849–1968

KEN GOOD

BOOKMARQUE
PUBLISHING

First published September 2002

British Library Cataloguing in Publication Data
A catalogue for this book is available from the British Library

ISBN 1-870519-67-1

This work is published with the assistance of the Michael Sedgwick Trust.
Founded in memory of the famous motoring author and researcher, Michael C. Sedgwick (1926-1983),
the Trust is a registered charity to encourage the publishing of new research and recording of motoring history.
Suggestions for future projects or donations should be sent to the Hon. Secretary of the Michael Sedgwick Trust,
c/o The National Motor Museum, Beaulieu, Hampshire SO42 7ZN United Kingdom.
Further details on www.sedgwicktrust.com

FRONT COVER:
*Painting by Pat Good of the seven Gwynne Eights which foregathered at the
Cornish home of Gwynne 'guru' Bill Cornock in 1993.
This first of a series of annual visits demonstrated justification for the claims made
in Gwynnes' original advertisement (see p.109).
Four of the cars had made a round trip of some 700 trouble free miles!*

FRONTISPIECE:
*The author leans proudly on his Gwynne Eight,
along with his wife, Pat, at the wheel.*

Set in 11 on 13pt Times
Printed on Fineblade 115 gsm
Published by Bookmarque Publishing
Printed in Great Britain by Antony Rowe Ltd

Contents

Preface

HARRY KENNETH GOOD retired from the Civil Service in 1982 having spent his life in his birthplace of Cardiff, in Italy and in London.

He retained his attachment to his family roots in Somerset and South Wales where he had been driven as a small boy in his grandfather's 1925 Gwynne Eight. Research of his family history after retirement uncovered family photographs of that Gwynne and he set about securing one to purchase. This he did in 1988—a 1923 Gwynne Eight (XO1866).

He utilised his unique talents in administration and communication to contact Gwynne owners in the UK and create the Gwynne Register. Lacking the necessary mechanical skills—he was always a 'word' man —he was grateful for the intervention of these vintage car experts for much of the restoration of his car.

Inspired by his purchase he applied himself (in the specific and meticutous manner that was so respected in his Civil Service days), to research of the Gwynnes. This led to the identification of all the surviving Gwynne cars (Alberts and Tens as well as Eights) and the publication of the quarterly *Gwynneformation* Circular which linked owners and other supporters and led to more widespread interest in and knowledge of the marque.

The assiduous research he did for the circular extended to details of the Gwynne family members and all their industrial concerns: fascinating for Gwynne owners! His own fascination with the historical facts encouraged him to write this book. Close to completion at the time of his sudden death his work has been finalised for publication by his wife, Pat, and family.

His interests were wide and motoring shared its place with classical music, rugby and Cardiff City Football Club—of which he was a lifelong supporter.

Ken Good's family

Ken

KEN had almost completed the text leaving just a few paragraphs on pumps for me to finish. It was all in good order but he had made no indication of which illustrations he would use. Selection and, more importantly, sourcing and attribution proved a major task. The pile of paper work that had accumulated over the years was at least three feet high. My family helped, particularly Nick who scanned and captioned in such spare time as he could find. I am grateful to them all and also to John Rose of Bookmarque Publishing whose patience with the endless deliberations over modernisation of punctuation was appreciated. Our desire was to honour Ken's original work and traditional style as closely as possible but eventually a compromise was reached. I think Ken would have acceded on these points.

We have no idea to whom Ken would have dedicated his book — I would like to look on it as a memorial to him and it is in that spirit that I have given so much of the last twelve months. It has been a comfort and I hope that he would be pleased with the end result.

Pat Good
Barnet, Herts. July 2002

Author's Introduction

MY INTEREST in Gwynnes came about when, on going through old family papers, I found photographs of XY-6017, the 1925 Gwynne Eight car which my grandfather had bought new from the Chiswick factory in London. I last saw it being used as a garage hack in Cardiff, my native City, around 1937. The photographs made me wonder whether any Gwynnes still existed.

From that stemmed my finding my own 1923 Gwynne Eight, my identifying over thirty Gwynne cars worldwide and the establishment of a formal Register at the wholehearted prompting of C. H. Peacock, its President, a life-long enthusiast for the marque. With each discovery of yet another Gwynne product my interest grew in learning more about the people who founded this part of British industrial history and in recording what became of them and their works. Hence this book.

In writing it I would like to pay particular tribute to three friends who are also owners of Gwynne cars for their contributions to and corrections of specific chapters. They are Ian Walker, David Woodburn and the late Professor Ian Smith. Not only have their contributions to the written word been invaluable but, without their unstinted help and guidance, I would never have been able to maintain and enjoy my splendid Gwynne Eight car.

Whilst a certain amount of basic information about individuals in the Gwynne family is readily available in the public domain, I have been extraordinarily fortunate in having been allowed to draw on a remarkable book about the family which was published as I was carrying out my research. This was *Violet: The Life and Loves of Violet Gordon Woodhouse* by Jessica Douglas-Home. The author and her subject are of the family of James Eglington Anderson Gwynne who played a profound and not always benevolent part in our story. I am most grateful to her for her kind permission for me to draw on her published work as background with which to flesh out my skeletal knowledge of the Gwynne family.

9

I am equally grateful to her brother, Nevile Martin Gwynne, the only surviving male descendant to bear the family name, for his deep interest and for all the information that he has given me. I am especially grateful for him so readily giving me permission to refer to the unpublished story of Nevile Gwynne's family, which was written by Mrs Katharine Ayling, Nevile's eldest daughter.

I must also thank Michael R. Lane for his ready agreement that I might refer to his monumental histories of The Queen's Engineering Works, Bedford and the Wellington Foundry, Lincoln. Both W. H. Allen and Sir William Tritton, the respective heads of those organisations, started their careers and remained intimately connected with Gwynnes throughout their working lives.

Finally I should say that any conclusions that I may reach in this narrative are entirely my own.

Kenneth Good
Barnet, Hertfordshire
January 2000

The 1925 Gwynne Eight that was owned by Ken Good's grandfather.

Chapter One

The House of Gwynne

THE GWYNNES first came into prominence in the first part of the 19th century as makers of centrifugal pumps. Designed initially to move water, they became used extensively for the drainage of and reclamation of land both in this country and, later, world wide. Many other uses would follow.

In the First World War, in addition to pumps, Gwynnes produced engines for combat aeroplanes used both by the Royal Naval Air Service and the Royal Flying Corps. They built on this experience after the war to manufacture motor cars. Fire-fighting equipment also formed part of their production.

After a slump in the family fortunes in the 1920s, the name of Gwynne and many of its products survived in other hands until as recently as 1968 when, in a series of amalgamations, the name and those of some of its successor companies disappeared. Some of the Gwynne designs for large centrifugal pumps are still in use today, however. It is the story of what started out as a small family business that we shall follow in this narrative.

Before setting out on the industrial trail I will delve first into the family background because, perhaps to an unusual extent, that influenced events, beginning with the earliest member of the family about whom anything is known.

WILLIAM GWYNNE (1775-1838)

Despite several attempts by members of his family to trace his origins, little is known about William. He is thought to have been descended from the Gwynnes of Glanbran, Llanfair-ar-y-Bryn, near Llandovery, Dyfed, though he may have been born in London. Of William's seven children only two need concern us here: John and George. John, as the founder of the first Gwynne business to achieve international fame is the one of primary concern to this history. The part that George played, though fundamental, can be briefly covered first.

GEORGE GWYNNE (1823-1873)

Like his brother John, George was of a mechanical bent though he trained as an analytical chemist. As a young man he emigrated to the Pittsburg area of USA where he was attracted to the potential of a primitive centrifugal pump, the principle of which is said to have been invented by a Frenchman, de Demour, in 1732. By 1844 George had built the first double entry balanced centrifugal pump and supplied it to the Passaic copper mine where it was a success. George also purchased the patent rights to an earlier centrifugal pump made by one W. D. Andrews for use in New York Harbour. After passing details to John, George returned to this country where, in 1845, he became a chemical technician with Prices Patent Candle Co. Ltd of Battersea, London. That rather prosaic title embraced a wide range of products including the well-known 'Motorine' brand of motor oils. George remained with the firm until his death and, over the years, took out many patents in connection with the distillation of fats.

JOHN GWYNNE I (1800-1855)

It was John I who, in 1849, founded the family firm on the basis of his brother's work. This he did on his return from Bushmills, Co. Antrim, Ireland, where he had been sent to study engineering at the works owned by other members of the family. In setting up his business John was helped financially by his friend Herbert Twining, the tea trader and merchant banker. So, from the outset, he concerned himself not only with manufacture but also, with Twining's advice, property investment. Thus the first factory in Essex Street, Aldwych, London, was chosen near Twining's business and in part for its potential value in the foreseeable development of the Thames Embankment.

Like his father, John had seven children, four of whom were to be involved in the business. They were James Eglington Anderson, a second John, Henry Anderson and another George. This George did not remain long because he became involved in some doubtful financial matters and so, to avoid scandal, it was decided that he should emigrate to Australia.

When John died at the relatively early age of 55, James, the eldest son who had worked with his father from the outset, took control of the business at the tender age of 23.

JAMES EGLINGTON ANDERSON GWYNNE (1831-1915)

We learn from Mrs Douglas-Home's book that, as a family, the male Gwynnes "ran to explosive tempers, a stubborn streak and considerable willpower". All these qualities came out in James when he was faced with the implacable hostility of his mother to his proposed marriage to Mary Earle Purvis, daughter of a wealthy Edinburgh family. Mary's mother, granddaughter of a Sumatran ranee, had been educated in India and described herself as "an Indian". Significantly for future events, no member of either the Gwynne family or his mother's Anderson family attended the wedding. As we shall see, that, and James's own authoritarian nature would lead to a division of the family firm with the two younger brothers setting up a rival pumps business, J. & H. Gwynne, with financial backing from their mother.

Nevertheless the original company, Gwynne & Co., continued to prosper. James was a man of wide interests. Not content with running the firm, he started a private supply of electricity in the Euston Road area in 1882. For this he linked Gwynne steam engines to Patterson & Cooper dynamos in Stanhope Street premises and, by means of overhead cables, supplied electricity to neighbouring concerns. He also devised his own telegraph company to send 'Gwynnegrams'. Like his father, James was involved in property development around the Law Courts and the fortune he made from all these activities was largely invested in purchases of land in that part of Sussex where he had made his home. For example, in 1876, he bought two manor houses,

Folkington and Wootton, about one mile apart. Prominent among other properties that he owned and partially restored was Michelham Priory.

Unhappily, as he grew richer, his interest in the business diminished so that much of the daily routine was left to his son, Nevile, as James increasingly played the part of the country squire. Nor was his home life rewarding; his stern moral code and morose, detached nature caused his wife and children to fear rather than warm towards him.

Like his father and grandfather before him, James had seven surviving children. All four sons and one of his three daughters were to achieve prominence though, as will be explained, this brought little pleasure to their father or, indeed, to most of them. The prominent children of James were:

REGINALD JOHN GWYNNE, CMG (1863-1942)

After Eton, from where he had to be removed for extravagance, Reginald went to Lancing College in Sussex. He subsequently went up to Oxford University where he incurred debts equivalent to over £120,000 in today's terms. As a result he was removed from Oxford and banished to Canada. There he joined the Army and, by 1911, had reached the rank of Brigadier-General. In 1914 he was appointed Director-General of Mobilisation in Canada and, in 1917, Adjutant-General. He was mentioned in despatches on three occasions. Despite his success he was never reconciled to or accepted by his father who, when the question of his return to this country was mooted, merely advised him to declare himself bankrupt. On retiring from the Army in 1921, Reginald settled in Canada with his wife and surviving daughter.

Thus, with his eldest son banished, James's hopes of continuing his industrial dynasty rested next on the shoulders of Nevile.

NEVILE GWYN GWYNNE, CBE (1868-1951)

Nevile was educated at Lancing and Pembroke College, Cambridge, where he was one of the first engineering graduates. On graduating he joined his father at the Essex Street works and, in 1892, when the move to Brooke Street, Holborn took place, he was appointed manager. In effect this was a position with responsibility but without authority.

14

Though his father's appearances at the works became increasingly rare, Nevile was not allowed to take decisions and often had difficulty in extracting his by no means generous salary from James. It could be that the tension arose because James detected something in Nevile's style of management of which he did not approve. Alternatively that he suspected Nevile had a tendency to take irrational decisions which, in little more than a decade, would result in the long-established and profitable business falling into other hands.

Matters came to a head in August 1903 when, after a violent quarrel, Nevile struck his father. That night James removed Nevile from his will as a beneficiary. Later, Nevile was effectively dismissed from his position as Gwynne & Co. had to be sold to J. & H. Gwynne. After the better part of a year without a position, Nevile joined the merged companies now controlled by his uncle, John II. There was not even a seat on the board for James. The breach was now total.

The depth of the differences between father and son is clear from an exchange of letters, which has subsequently been seen. On 23 October 1903, after the devastating quarrel which so affected the lives of the whole family for generations to come, James wrote his son a letter in which he expressed the view that engineering was not to Nevile's taste or liking and that he had not made a success of it; that the constant worry and anxiety which he (James) had endured had come about since the business had been under Nevile's management and that his instructions and wishes had not been carried out. Finally he declared that he would not put capital into a business which had proved such a financial failure since Nevile had had its management. This was a devastating message for a father to convey to his son and shows James to have been totally lacking in sensitivity and, indeed, in any paternal feeling.

In Nevile's defence it must be said that it had been many years since his father had been to the works, that he had lost touch with or interest in the rapidly developing engineering environment and that he had steadfastly refused to heed Nevile's repeated advice to modernise the plant to face the increasing loss of business particularly to the rival Gwynne firm of John and Henry at Hammersmith. There is abundant evidence that James was utterly unreasonable in his reactions to any demand made on his considerable wealth whether of a personal or a business nature.

On the death of John II in 1912, Nevile became Managing Director of the combined family firm of Gwynnes Ltd, Hammersmith, London.

Nevile Gwyn Gwynne photographed with General Manager, Mr W. Cannell, and King Edward VII during his visit to the Chiswick works in 1917.

Nevile Gwyn Gwynne walking with King Edward VII.

Married to Isabel Violet (daughter of Admiral Charles Wake, RN) he had one son and three daughters. He was a Member of the Institutions of Mechanical Engineers and Naval Architects and Vice-President of the Federation of British Industries (now the CBI).

Nevile's son, John Nevile Wake Gwynne (1905-1981) broke with the family tradition of engineering by becoming a solicitor and company secretary. He inherited Nether Stowey Manor from his aunt Violet Gordon Woodhouse and lived there until his death in 1981. John had two children, a son and a daughter. The son, Nevile Martin Gwynne, is a retired chartered account-ant who lives in Ireland. He is in regular correspondence with the Gwynne Register which records the history of the cars which his grandfather made. It was the daughter, now Mrs Jessica Douglas-Home, who wrote the fascinating book *Violet* about her aunt.

RUPERT SACKVILLE GWYNNE, MP (1873-1924)

After education at Shrewsbury and Pembroke College, Cambridge, Rupert was called to the Bar at the Inner Temple in 1908 and two years later was elected MP for Eastbourne. In 1923 and 1924, until his untimely death at the age of 51, he served as Financial Secretary to the War Office. In 1905 Rupert had married the Hon. Stella Ridley, a daughter of the first Viscount Ridley who was Home Secretary from 1895 to 1900 in Lord Salisbury's administration.

Rupert had a weak heart as a result of his having contracted rheumatic fever as a youth. Even so, and despite warnings to the contrary, he led the extremely active life of a country gentleman. He played no part in the family business. Given the terms of James's will, which passed the inheritance down the male line to safeguard the business and the family, it was ironic that, with Rupert's death, that inheritance should pass to Roland, the youngest son. This was as a direct result of James's intemperate treatment of his two older sons.

One of Rupert's four daughters achieved lasting fame as Mrs Elizabeth David who, almost single-handedly, did so much to raise the culinary standards of this country both domestically and professionally.

SIR ROLAND VAUGHAN GWYNNE, DSO, DL, JP (1882-1971)

Educated privately and at Trinity Hall, Cambridge, Roland was called to the Bar at Inner Temple in 1910. He practised in the Probate and Divorce Division. In the First World War, as Lt. Col. Gwynne, he commanded the Queen's Royal West Surrey Regiment with which he was twice wounded, mentioned in despatches and awarded the DSO for bravery at Ypres. Roland was High Sheriff for Sussex 1926/27, Mayor of Eastbourne from 1928 to 1931, Chairman of the East Sussex County Council from 1937 to 1940 and Chairman of the Justices for many years.

Roland's upbringing was largely ignored by his father. A homosexual, he was regarded as scheming and dishonourable by all the family save his mother and his sister Violet. Despite his glowing record of public service, for which he was knighted, Roland grew increasingly dissolute as he aged with the result that he was blackmailed by his butler among others. Even so on his death at the age of 90, attended in his last illness by the notorious Dr Bodkin Adams (who was later to be acquitted of charges of having murdered several rich and terminally ill patients), Roland's gross effects amounted to the equivalent of £1.7m in current terms. None of this reached the family: all was left to Roland's friend, Sir Dingwall Latham Bateson, to administer according to his (Roland's) expressed wishes.

VIOLET GORDON WOODHOUSE (1871-1948)

The only one of James's daughters to achieve prominence, Violet became famous as a musician but notorious for her life-style in that she lived harmoniously in a *ménage a cinq*. As an artiste she was, in fact, the first ever to be recorded playing the harpsichord and her salons were attended by virtually all the famous names of the first half of the 20th Century. Friend of Delius, Sir Thomas Beecham, the Sitwells, Dolmetsch and Diaghilev among others, Violet was largely responsible for the revival of interest in the music of Domenico Scarlatti.

Returning to their father, James, it is clear that his many and varied interests had been highly profitable. When he died on 22 March 1915 at his Folkington Manor home, James's effects were valued at £233,493 (over £8m at today's value). He left a life interest in his house and estates to his wife and in the Home Farm estate to his unmarried daughter, Dorothy Blanche. He bequeathed all his lands in Canada to Reginald but specifically excluded him from any inheritance in this country. Roland was given the Michelham estate and the residual rights to his several other farms and estates were left to Rupert. In all, James's estates comprised some 8,000 acres and it was said locally that "you could hunt all day on Squire Gwynne's lands without coming to the end".

But, by his behaviour as the archetypal heavy Victorian father and by the terms of his will, James had brought about the total disintegration of the very family that he sought to protect. Reginald was banished to Canada; Nevile was disinherited and, through suspicion that his lawyer brother Rupert had influenced their father over the terms of the will, was no longer on speaking terms with his brother; Roland was devious and mistrusted by almost everyone. Of the daughters, Evelyn's husband, Charles Isaacson, became bankrupt and she died childless and in poverty before the First World War. Dorothy seems to have spent her spinsterhood thwarted in her love for Violet's husband,

Gordon Woodhouse. In fact, of James's seven children, it would seem that only Violet was universally loved and admired.

Most significantly, however, none of James's considerable fortune of over £8m at current values could be used to further the business interests of the family. Most of it was squandered by Roland, who lived in lavish style at Folkington Manor until he was forced in later life to move back to the relatively more modest Wootton Manor which had been the home of Rupert and his family.

JOHN GWYNNE II (1838-1912)
and
HENRY ANDERSON GWYNNE (died 1889)

As already mentioned, John II and Henry the younger brothers of James, joined him in their father's firm, John as an apprentice in 1853. In time they found irksome the fact that they were allowed so little say in running the business. Eventually, with their mother's help, they started the rival firm of J. & H. Gwynne in Hammersmith in 1868. Given John's eminence as an engineer and James's gradual withdrawal from day-to-day operations at Gwynne and Co., it is hardly surprising to find that the new firm soon outstripped the original.

It would seem that Henry's role was a minor one and that, around 1882, he became interested in a paper mill in Hertfordshire. Soon he was little more than a sleeping partner having begun to show signs of mental instability. When he died in a mental home in 1889, his widow sought release from the partnership. In typical Gwynne fashion, however, John was prepared to incur the costs of going to Court rather than reach agreement privately. It seems that he had taken a strong dislike to Henry's widow. The outcome was that arbitrators appointed by the Courts of Chancery awarded Henry's widow and her co-executors the sum of £26,122 as his share of the business. John also paid back the loan that his mother had advanced to start the business.

An interesting sidelight was thrown on the intense rivalry of the Gwynne siblings by a document found in the Lincolnshire County Record Office. In 1957, one of Henry's granddaughters wrote to Mr Henry Humphreys, a Director of Allen Gwynnes Pumps, Ltd (a company whose place in the scheme of things will be made clear later) to say that her mother was ill and without means. She appealed to the firm for help not realising that it no longer had any connection with the family. In passing the plea to another Director, Mr Humphreys, a friend of the family for many years, commented:

> The whole story is very involved and really nothing to do with us... ...through the whole history of the Gwynne family there seem to have been plenty of squabbles about money matters...

John died at his home, Kenton Grange, Harrow, London, on 2 May 1912. A widower, he had no children. His effects were valued at £40,652. After several bequests to his housekeeper, his first and second coachmen and 'each indoor and outdoor servant' he left the residue in trust for two daughters of his brother and partner, Henry. Another daughter received a small lump sum.

Once again, significantly, no bequest was made to Nevile who, by this time had worked with his uncle for nearly ten years. Deservedly or not he had, of course, received nothing from his father's estate and, on his mother's death, his own brothers would do nothing to remedy the situation. It is only fair to add that Rupert did attempt to create a scheme whereby each of the siblings would renounce his or her claim to the inheritance in favour of a settlement of money. All seemed to be agreed in principle until sister Dorothy was refused a sum of money from the estate towards repairs to her property. She thereupon declined to have any part in the scheme and it collapsed. However, Nevile was now in sole control of the unified family concern and subsequent chapters illustrate how he fared in that role.

* * *

The GWYNNE Family Members mentioned in this narrative

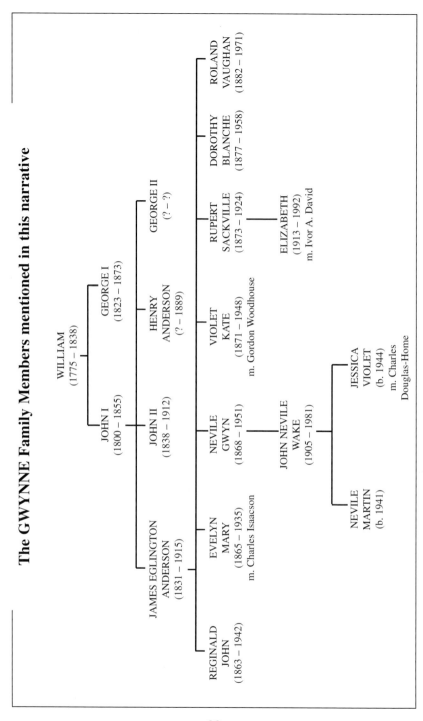

Chapter Two

The Companies called Gwynne

THE ROLES of the eight companies which bore the name 'Gwynne' or 'Gwynnes' in their titles shall now be considered. Interestingly not all of them were businesses run by or even connected to the founding family.

Gwynne & Co.

This was the original company founded by John Gwynne I (1800-1855) in 1849 at Essex Street, Aldwych, London for the manufacture of centrifugal pumps. In this he took forward the development by his brother George of the French invention. By 1850 John had produced the first multi-stage version, the patent for which was issued to him on 31 March 1851. This was the first example of a type now in general use.

In that year John exhibited several pumps at the Great Exhibition in Hyde Park, London. Two competitors following similar lines also appeared. They were J. G. Appold, a consulting civil engineer and a Mr Bessemer. Although the bearer of an illustrious name, little is known about Bessemer. The first application of a centrifugal pump to fen drainage followed when an order for an Appold pump was placed with Messrs Easton and Anderson of London. John Gwynne immediately issued a challenge to the effect that his pump would prove the more efficient in use. The challenge, involving a stake of £1,000 each, was not taken up.

The business expanded after demonstrations at the Exhibition so that a new works became necessary. This was provided in 1852 about one hundred yards west of the original premises. The iron foundry was situated separately in Parker Street off Holborn Kingsway, London.

In 1855 John died after a mere six years in charge of the business that he founded. His eldest son, James, became the managing partner and his younger sons, John II and Henry, also joined the undertaking. Having failed to buy adjoining premises in the area of the Thames Embankment for further expansion, James sold the Essex Wharf site to James Astor at a considerable profit and bought premises in Brooke Street, Holborn. This site proved to be far from ideal in that not only was it cramped but it was distant from the rail and water transport needed to bring raw materials in and to take finished products out. Worse still it lacked the abundant water supply needed for testing pumps.

Even so James arranged for a trial to be conducted at the 1862 International Exhibition at Battersea, London by Mr Zerah Colbourn, founder and editor of the trade magazine, *The Engineer*. This was to establish the relative efficiency of the Gwynne pump in competition with that made by the well-known engineering partnership of Easton, Amos & Sons, who had by then been joined by Bessemer. Colbourn's report of 22 November of that year found that the efficiency of the Gwynne pump exceeded that of the Easton by 16%.

After the brothers John and Henry broke away to form another firm of Gwynne pump makers at Hammersmith, this original company continued to prosper. The summary of accounts for 1888, for example, showed a gross profit of £5,267 and net profit of £2,926 on sales of £17,958. There is some evidence, however, that it always lagged behind the Hammersmith company particularly in land drainage equipment. Regrettably it is clear that the brothers were fiercely competitive even to the extent of taking orders against one another out of pique rather than on a sound business basis.

J. & H. Gwynne

John II and Henry had become increasingly resentful at being confined to relatively minor roles in the business by the dictatorial James. Moreover, they were convinced that more could be done to improve the pumps. Their mother supported them as they had backed her in her opposition to James's proposed marriage. In April 1858 she lent them £7,000 to buy land and erect new works on the banks of the Thames at Hammersmith.

Staff at J. & H. Gwynne, Engineers, Crisp Road, Hammersmith c. 1880. Reproduced by kind permission of the Hammersmith and Fulham Archives and Local History Centre.

25

The first entry in the Hammersmith Borough Council rate books shows the works to have been established on the site of Riverside House in Queen's Road (now Crisp Road), London, W6. This, in the names of George and Henry Gwynne, is for October 1867. It is not clear why John's name did not appear and even more puzzling is the reappearance of George. Possibly as he had a settled salaried post he was regarded as a more appropriate nominee. By April 1872, the Gwynnes also owned Nos. 8 to 12 Queen's Road and, in nearby Chancellor Street, a room over the gateway of No. 2 and a workshop. The riverside location of the main premises overcame all the disadvantages of the Brooke Street site.

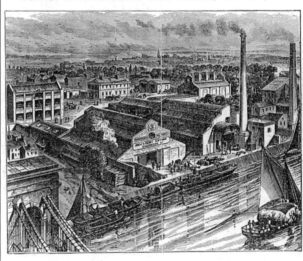

John and Henry Gwynne Engineers Catalogue of Centrifugal Pumps and other machinery, 1876.

JOHN & HENRY GWYNNE,

ENGINEERS,

OFFICES: 89, CANNON STREET, LONDON, E.C.

WORKS: HAMMERSMITH IRON WORKS, LONDON, W.

CATALOGUE

OF

CENTRIFUGAL PUMPS, PUMPING MACHINES,

AND OTHER MACHINERY.

At Hammersmith John designed the equipment while Henry was responsible for outdoor installation. In a publication *Land Drainage* in 1943, Gwynnes Pumps, Ltd (by then long owned by William Foster, Ltd of Lincoln) said that John Gwynne was responsible for all the advances in centrifugal pump design in his time while the design of his steam engines showed him to be head and shoulders above his contemporaries.

On 1 May 1897 J. & H. Gwynne became a limited liability company under the style of J. & H. Gwynne, Ltd. As a concern they by no means confined their activities to pumps but competed for general engineering projects. The most notable of these was the construction of an Inclined Plane to replace the series of thirteen locks on the Grand Union Canal at Foxton in Leicestershire. Gwynne's estimate for machines and steelwork was successful at £14,630. This was so for various technical reasons despite its being more costly than those of its competitors. The Plane was operational from 1900 to 1910 when it was adjudged to be uneconomic to keep the boiler in steam all day. Much of the structure was sold as scrap for £250 in 1928 but enough remains to this day to give an impression of the scale of the undertaking.

Gwynnes, Ltd

Some knowledge has now been gained of the family dissension against which, through the intervention of Henry Marshall of Gainsborough, one of the arbitrators in the dispute over the inheritance of Henry's widow, a Memorandum of Agreement for amalgamation dated 12 June 1903 was signed. John bought out James for an agreed price of £29,500. The Brooke Street site was sold to the Prudential Assurance Co. Ltd and the unified firm of Gwynnes, Ltd was registered at Hammersmith Iron Works in August 1903.

Nevile, the second son of James, having quarrelled irreconcilably with his father, joined his uncle on the Board. John acted as Managing Director of the company from its inception until he resigned in May 1911. He was succeeded by Nevile who had been appointed assistant to the Managing Director on 24 June 1903. John remained as Chairman and was appointed as consultant engineer. There was no place for James in the new company even had he wished it: he had long lost interest in the business. The other Director was J. G. Mair-Rumley. Following the death of John on 2 May 1912 at the age of 74, Nevile assumed sole control of the amalgamated family business.

Gwynnes Ltd Engineering Works from Hammersmith Bridge.
Reproduced by kind permission of the Hammersmith and Fulham Archives and Local History Centre.

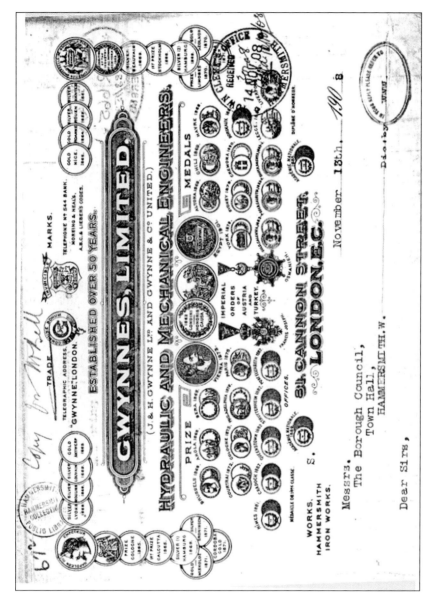

Letter headings from the early twentieth-century.
Reproduced by kind permission of the Hammersmith and Fulham Archives and Local History Centre.

By August 1914, on the outbreak of the First World War, Gwynnes had capital of £82,000 and debentures of £30,350 which were subsequently redeemed. But, with the onset of the conflict, they had no orders. Within a few months, however, the Admiralty had placed orders for pumping machinery and had also approached the firm to undertake the manufacture of a new 100 hp rotary aeroplane engine. At first Gwynnes demurred because of the shortage of skilled workers, their inexperience in this field and their weak financial position. But, given financial assurances and an exclusive licence, they rented part of the old Thornycroft shipyards at Church Wharf, Chiswick, London and set about the tasks of acquiring the necessary machinery and of recruiting and training the workforce. Eventually the entire works of some 250,000 sq.ft. was commandeered and substantially rebuilt. Gwynnes purchased the freehold in 1916 to retain the site value for the company. Initially some 1,200 men and 800 women were employed but, as the war progressed, those proportions were reversed. Among the employees were Nevile Gwynne's three daughters, one of whom worked in the accounts department while the other two were 'getting their hands dirty'. The wages bill at times exceeded £9,000 weekly.

In all, Gwynnes, together with Ruston, Proctor, Ltd of Lincoln, their sub-licensees, made some 3,600 Clerget engines at a cost of £3.6m. by January 1920. Their total profit on the business was £497,000 but, as their pre-war standard of profit was no more than £7,500, some £420,000 was claimed back by the Exchequer in the form of Excess Profit Duty. Of this some £200,000 was paid, but the outstanding balance was never agreed with Inland Revenue although further sums were paid.

When peace was restored, Gwynnes anticipated a flourishing market for the development of civil and military aviation. But no government support was forthcoming and so they accepted the only logical alternative for their engine plant which was the manufacture of motor car engines. About June 1919 they agreed a contract for engines for the new Albert car and so they placed firm orders for materials for these chassis amounting to over £400,000. Subsequently when its makers, Adam, Grimaldi of Glasshouse Street (now Walk), Vauxhall, London, proved unable to pay for the first batch of rolling chassis delivered,

Gwynnes decided to purchase the issued capital of the firm for a consideration of £57,251. The purchase was completed in March 1920.

The financial consequences of the national strike of foundry moulders from October 1919 to February 1920 were increases in stock held at Chiswick and Vauxhall to the value of £239,000 and £29,000 respectively.

All these events led to a need for further capital but the company's bankers advised them that, mainly because of the unresolved Excess Profits Duty claim, it was not practicable to raise capital in the markets to finance the contracts undertaken. To obtain additional capital therefore, the Board decided to sell all the company's property (other than cash in hand and book debts) as at 1 January 1920 to a new company to be called Gwynnes Engineering Co. Ltd. The purchase price was fixed at £575,000 of which £225,000 was in cash and the balance of £350,000 in fully paid-up £1 shares. This included the issued capital of Adam, Grimaldi & Co. Ltd.

In 1921, the Directors of Gwynnes, Ltd were J. M. Dewar, an engineer, and M. A. Edwards, the company's solicitor, while those of Gwynnes Engineering Co. Ltd were A. G. Cousins, W. W. Weekes, the company secretary, and Dewar. Nevile Gwynne was the Managing Director of both companies. This does seem to have been a cosy arrangement.

On 20 January 1921 the Board of Gwynnes, Ltd attempted to present its report and balance sheet to a meeting of shareholders in overall terms to cover the period from 1 February 1916 to 30 September 1920. This was strongly opposed by several members who demanded annual audited accounts for each year showing salaries and Directors' fees with that of the Managing Director, Nevile himself, separately. The proposal was narrowly defeated on the grounds that there were outstanding questions on various government contracts and on the resolution of the Excess Profits Duty problem.

This rejection might be considered somewhat surprising since the net profits of the company year by year had been certified and reported in the trade press by March 1920. What had the Board to hide? A key might be found in one of the reasons given by Mr Gwynne for Excess Profits Duty being so high. This was that the company wrote off more

THE HOUSE OF GWYNNE

in depreciation on buildings, plant, leases and loose tools (though not on stock) than was allowed by Inland Revenue. Although depreciation is an account book transaction, it does reduce the profit for distribution as dividend to shareholders. Could this 'paper expenditure' have concealed excess remuneration to the Directors, details of which Mr Gwynne resolutely refused to divulge?

Several attempts were made by shareholders to force a committee of enquiry into financial aspects but all were defeated by the Board, some on a technicality. Significantly one shareholder complained that he could never get information when he wrote to the Board and that the Board had been badly advised on financial matters.

One could not help wondering how, when the company was in so parlous a state financially and when, as we know, Mr Gwynne had inherited nothing from either his rich father or his wealthy uncle, he was able around this time to purchase an estate of some 360 acres near the family home in Sussex; this in addition to his Town house in a Kensington square.

It has been learned from family sources that Mr Gwynne emerged from the First World War a very rich man, the expression 'millionaire' was used by one grandson, and this is more than borne out if the total of his remuneration as Managing Director of Gwynnes, Ltd for the years 1914 to 1920 as shown in the Statement of Affairs at the time of the voluntary liquidation is translated into equivalent contemporary values. It could be that this clouding of accounts was an attempt to prevent such information from reaching the public domain. It is also said that he lost much of his wealth when, after learning that other Directors were secretly selling shares, he set about buying them in so as to keep control of the firm. There is no doubt, too, that he put a great deal of money from his personal fortune into trying to compete with the major car companies with their huge capital resources. But this is to look ahead.

The detail of Gwynnes Engineering Co. Ltd will shortly be considered but, in the meantime, Gwynnes, Ltd continued its separate existence as creditor of and largest shareholder in that company. For the period from 1 February 1916 to 30 September 1920 the Directors recommended a dividend of 5% on the Preference and 10% on the

Ordinary shares leaving a balance of £46,980 on the Profit and Loss Account to be carried forward. A similar dividend was proposed for the following year and a further loan of £24,000 was made to Gwynnes Engineering, Ltd.

By 31 December 1922, the credit balance stood at £92,890 after completion of the adjustments of account left over from the war. No monies had been received by way of repayment from Gwynnes Engineering, Ltd. but the shareholders' meeting was told that there was *"...every likelihood of an improvement in that firm's position."* No dividend was proposed. Gwynnes, Ltd was, of course, no longer a manufacturing concern.

The last official reference we have been able to trace of Gwynnes, Ltd is the report of the Annual Meeting held on 12 May 1924. Apart from some good news about the disposal of some stock of aeroplane engines and spares, everything was held in abeyance pending the outcome of the restructuring of Gwynnes Engineering Co. Ltd to which a Receiver and Manager had been appointed on 6 July 1923 on behalf of the debenture holders. At that Annual Meeting the liquidation of both the Adam, Grimaldi and Lang Propellers subsidiaries was announced.

Gwynnes Engineering Co. Ltd

This company was incorporated on 23 March 1920 with a nominal capital of £600,000 in Ordinary shares of £1 each. Of these, 350,000 were allotted to Gwynnes, Ltd in part payment of the purchase price of £575,000, the balance being offered for subscription. In addition there was £300,000 of debenture stock. As part of the deal, Gwynnes Engineering should have paid £225,000 in cash. That, however, could only be raised by turning stocks of parts into cars and selling them. In the slump of 1920 that had become increasingly difficult particularly because the early Albert cars were developing a poor reputation.

The theory behind the creation of the new company was that because Gwynnes, Ltd had no cash capital and had more liabilities than assets, except in buildings, plant and machinery, the best known method by which those assets could be converted into cash was by sale to a new company. The new company did not acquire the whole of Gwynnes, Ltd in that it did not take over the liabilities. On the other hand it seemed to create its own liabilities from the outset.

The strike by foundry moulders from October 1919 to February 1920 meant that the factory was without engine castings. Further problems were experienced nationally from the body builders with the result that Gwynnes were left with a large stock of unusable chassis. It was found impossible to reorganise the former Adam, Grimaldi factory in time to turn out a corresponding number of bodies or to buy them in from elsewhere. As a result a substantial number of employees had to be laid off in that year. To safeguard its future position, Gwynnes used some of the capital newly released to purchase a controlling interest in Ealing Park Foundry and Lang Propellers of Weybridge in Surrey. The first ensured a supply of engine castings and the second essential supplies of wood and staff capable of fabricating car body frames. These were acquired in April 1920.

The first report covering the period from 1 January 1920 to 31 August 1921 was presented to the shareholders of the company on 4 November 1921. It showed a loss on the trading account of £103,164. After payment of interest, repairs and renewals and writing off £82,242 for depreciation, a deficit of £351,886 was left to be carried forward. The assets were currently valued at £663,332.

In the case of the pumps business, in January 1920 Gwynnes had more orders on their books than at any time in their history. Whilst orders were not cancelled, because of delivery delays brought about by the moulders' strike, new orders could not be obtained at the increased prices enforced by higher production costs.

As to cars, on 1 January 1920, the date of its taking over, the company had firm orders, with deposits, for 3,000 of the Albert and the in-house production capacity to match. The need to place large orders for scarce materials such as cylinder castings, chassis forging, timber and aluminium, together with erratic supplies, meant that stocks of part-completed cars built up: only some 400 of the 3,000 cars ordered were completed in 1920. The introduction of the improved G2 model exacerbated the situation by causing many of the superseded parts in stock to be discarded. This affected profits as did the cut of £100 in the selling price forced by increased competition: hence the trading loss.

There is little doubt that the Albert was uncompetitive in its 1.5 litre class. By 1921, Gwynnes had reduced its price to £495 for the two or four-seater, but the Morris Cowley, also 11.9 hp though with a side valve engine and a three speed gearbox, was available for only £375 and £425 respectively. The difference reflected the benefit of William Morris's policy of buying-in economically from established specialists as against Gwynne's policy of self-containment.

It is worth comment that in the company's annual report nothing but praise was lavished on the Albert car, the G3 model of which was about to be introduced. Yet one of the first actions of the Receiver and Manager who was to be appointed eighteen months later was to scrap the marque. With hindsight the sense of complacency at this share-holders' meeting was overpowering.

The trading account for 1922 recorded a profit of £193. The balance sheet, however, revealed a deficit of £126,637 which increased the overall figure to £478,545 after depreciation, debenture interest, interest on a bank loan and interest to Gwynnes, Ltd of £21,443. Once again the considerable expense of revaluation of assets was incurred despite the company's financial position. As a result assets were written down from £663,322 to £619,138 at constant values.

Despite the serious trade depression overall, especially on the pumps side, the 14hp Gwynne-Albert was introduced. To quote the Chairman's annual report, this was:

...to meet public demand for a car of greater power to seat five...
...and an 8hp car tested on the Continent has been adapted for manufacture in England. This little car has already attracted considerable attention by the remarkable results obtained in performance and very great expectations are entertained for its future.

This is the first reference to the Gwynne Eight in company papers. No mention has been found of the costs involved in the purchase of the design or on its development. Could this really have been the time to incur the costs of tooling-up for the new larger Fourteen and for purchasing and developing the smaller Eight? One has to question the competence of Mr Gwynne and his financial advisers in doing so against the background of so large an accumulated deficit and with little or no profit coming in from either side of the business for several years. One could also wonder at Mr Gwynne's engineering acumen in persisting with the development of the unsuccessful and unprofitable Albert car.

All the fine words in the previous annual report soon proved to be little more than a typical eulogy of a Chairman. On 26 June 1923 a petition was heard at the Companies Winding-up Court brought by the Dunlop Rubber Co. Ltd for the compulsory liquidation of Gwynnes Engineering. Gwynnes asked for a stay of execution as a scheme of reconstruction was being prepared for approval by a committee of creditors. By 21 July of that year, however, Mr John Davie, chartered accountant of Messrs. Goddard, Dunkley, Davie and Fryer of 3 London Wall Buildings, London, EC2 was appointed Receiver and Manager on behalf of debenture holders.

By 11 August 1923 the Dunlop petition and that of Gwynnes Engineering for the compulsory liquidation of Adam, Grimaldi, Ltd were before the Court. Gwynne's lawyer explained that Adam, Grimaldi was a sub-company of Gwynnes Engineering formed to work certain motor patents. Unfortunately it had not been successful in financial matters with the result that Gwynnes also got into trouble. The reconstruction scheme in course of preparation would separate the two companies. Deferment was again granted and this also enabled an action brought by a debenture holder to be stalled.

On 5 November of that year Gwynnes Engineering announced that financial facilities had been obtained to resume production of the Gwynne Fourteen and Gwynne Eight at the rate of 50 cars a week, the Receiver having abandoned the Albert.

It is interesting to record that under the banner headline of *The famous GWYNNE Cars in Production again*, the firm's full page advertisement, which must have been approved by the Receiver, appeared in the trade press. Its text began:

> The famous... ...cars are once more in full production. Happily the little problems of production have been solved and the cars have been greatly improved in many ways.

No mention of the real problems, of course, but as the company was in Receivership, its cars could not appear at the Motor Show under the rules of the Society of Motor Manufacturers and Traders who organised the Show.

It was not until April 1924 that the financial reconstruction scheme was finally tabled. Briefly this provided that:

- all unsecured creditors abstain from enforcing claims for six months but stay as creditors for the full amount;
- Gwynnes, Ltd, creditors for £371,195, accept 10/- (shillings) in the pound (£) in the form of paid-up shares and forgo £62,000 in interest; and,
- petitions presented to the Court be dismissed.

This was agreed given that the debt to Gwynnes, Ltd was more than twice that of all the other creditors together and that, since the Receiver was appointed, the company had run at a small profit largely due to economies effected. The business, the Receiver reported, was now in an even more healthy state. The average monthly sales had been substantially increased and orders were in hand for more than £80,000.

The scheme was sanctioned in the Chancery Division in May 1924. In May 1925 it was announced that, because of the continued ill-health of Mr John Davie, he would be succeeded as Receiver and Manager by Mr Herbert Esden.

Mr Esden, having already disposed of the car side, reported to the shareholders on 31 March 1926 on his efforts to sell the Hammersmith pump business. In his view this should have been capable of being run at a profit in normal conditions. There remained to be satisfied the bank's Prior Lien charge of £20,000 from February 1922 and the £19,000 which he had had to borrow to continue to trade.

He said that there were three courses open for the business:

- sell it as a going concern either as a whole or without the premises and machinery with those being sold subsequently;
- close down the business and sell the assets for whatever they would fetch; or,

THE HOUSE OF GWYNNE

- carry on the business and endeavour to reconstruct preferably with a concern manufacturing a similar class of product.

There was a likelihood of loss from taking the first course and a certainty of heavy loss in the second case. He would, therefore, continue to seek amalgamation with another company.

The Official Receiver said that the company seemed to have been in financial difficulties since its incorporation. Its failure was due to the disorganisation of production attributable to the strike of moulders of some years back, to the lack of demand for the Albert car following on certain inherent defects which made themselves manifest in the original models and to insufficient capital. He also commented that mismanagement had been a contributory cause of the failure.

On 4 February 1927, the Receiver and Manager announced the registration of a new company by name of Gwynnes Pumps, Ltd and on 12 February the sale of the assets of that side of Gwynnes Engineering Co. Ltd to Messrs William Foster & Co. Ltd of Lincoln for £52,000. The sale was formally completed on 13 April of that year. As part of the transaction Mr Gwynne and Mr C.V. Armitage, the works manager, were to be Directors of Fosters.

Gwynnes Engineering Co. Ltd was wound up by Court order in October 1926, removed from the Companies Register in March 1932 and formally dissolved on 17 August 1934 when a notice to that effect was posted in the London Gazette.

ASSOCIATED AND SUBSIDIARY COMPANIES

Before considering Gwynnes (1926), Ltd we should look briefly at the subordinate companies of Gwynnes Engineering Co. Ltd.

Adam, Grimaldi & Co. Ltd

This firm was incorporated in February 1917. It was taken over by Gwynnes, Ltd on 1 January 1920. In April 1925 the company was formally liquidated on the petition of Gwynnes Engineering Co. Ltd who were creditors in the sum of £114,457.

The company was first registered with a nominal capital of £10,000 to enter into an agreement with Brown, Hughes and Strachan, Ltd and its liquidator to manufacture and deal in motor cars, cycles, etc. The company acquired plant, stock and contracts for £1,200 and the lease of premises in Netherwood Road, Hammersmith, London. In April 1918, the company bought new works at Glasshouse Street (now Walk), Albert Embankment, Vauxhall, London, SE11, on the basis of personal loans from its Directors. To extend the premises a bank loan was guaranteed by those Directors. In October 1919, the firm became a limited liability company by which time the nominal capital had increased to £100,000.

Towards the end of that year the company entered into an agreement with Gwynnes for the supply of 3,000 chassis for which they would make bodies. By the time Gwynnes had a number of chassis ready for delivery, however, the company could not pay for them and so Gwynnes entered into negotiations to take over the company. By June 1923, the company was indebted to Gwynnes to the extent of £152,750 to reduce which a bank loan of £30,000 was obtained. In addition to the debt to Gwynnes Engineering, Ltd., the company also owed £9,908 to Gwynnes, Ltd and £2,416 to Lang Propellers, Ltd.

The Official Receiver said that, after a profit of £2,918 for the year ending March 1918, the following four years showed losses totalling £110,393. The total deficit including that to shareholders amounted to £205,211 with minimal assets largely used to defray the bank loan. The failure was due to lack of capital, heavy expenses in adapting the Albert Embankment premises and heavy overhead charges.

One is given to wonder what possessed Gwynnes' Directors and their financial advisers in allowing their company to become involved with one of such doubtful stability in the first place. Not only that but Gwynnes themselves later had to spend yet more money on re-organising the Albert works for the efficient production of car bodies.

An interesting aside appeared in the trade journal *Motor Commerce* on 7 July 1923 to the effect that:

Ernest Grimaldi & Co., Ltd., automobile agents of 87 Great Portland Street, London, having had brought to their notice that their business is being confused with that of Adam, Grimaldi, Ltd. against which a petition for compulsory liquidation has been filed, wish it to be known that they have no connection whatsoever with that firm.

The following year Grimaldi announced that he had severed connection with the firm which bore his name and was '...now disposed to consider a suitable appointment'. On 30 October 1926, there appeared in the same journal the news that Mr Ernest Grimaldi:

> ...who will be remembered by the trade for his connection with Adam, Grimaldi & Co. some time ago, has terminated his agreement with the Fellows Magneto Co. as sales manager and is open to consider any suitable appointment.

The expression about organising a party in a brewery comes to mind. And this was the man to whose firm Gwynnes tied their future!

Ealing Park Foundry

In April 1920, Gwynnes Engineering acquired a controlling interest in this business because "...largely in consequence of the protracted strike of moulders...we could not get castings anywhere in this country". By the end of the year they had reorganised it and installed up-to-date plant. The foundry was situated in the area known as Little Ealing at Junction Road off Windmill Road, London, W5. The area is still heavily populated and, over the years, complaints in the local press about noise and fumes were legion. Nonetheless the foundry was still active in 1949/50 latterly as part of the Qualcast-Biomid organisation. The only trace there is of Gwynnes formal participation in the management is that Nevile Gwynne's son-in-law, Mr A. E. de Burgh Jennings, was the Secretary and a Director of the foundry. No record of when Gwynnes disposed of the business has been found.

Lang Propellers, Ltd

Gwynnes' association with Langs of Weybridge, Surrey, presumably began with the manufacture, during the First World War, of the Clerget rotary aero engine. This company was also acquired in April 1920 after the fresh injection of capital. Presumably after the First World War scarce raw materials were made available by quota as was the case after 1945. By purchasing Lang, Gwynnes could acquire not only its quota of timber for body frames but also its skilled workforce to supplement the still inadequate Albert works output. Lang's liquidation was reported on 12 May 1924 though, in fact, the works closed in 1922.

Gwynnes (1926), Ltd

In the normal way such a title would refer to the reconstruction of a company after the liquidation of the original firm. This title appears in the indexes at Companies House and in the Public Record Office but there is no trace of any relevant papers. One can only suppose that it was intended to be used at some stage in the take-over of the pumps side by Fosters but that it was eventually decided that a more positive approach would be to use the meaningful title of Gwynnes Pumps, Ltd.

Gwynne Cars, Ltd

The sale of the cars side by the Receiver and Manager was confirmed by a Memorandum from Gwynnes Engineering Co. Ltd dated 8 July 1925, to the effect that Mr Nevile Gwynne had taken control as from 1 May that year. In detail he had bought all the Church Wharf properties and the assets and goodwill of the motor car business for £77,500. This was done with the full approval of the Court as the best course available in the interest of the debenture holders. Surprisingly, the sum involved proved to be considerably more than was later to be obtained for the far more famous and long-established pumps business.

Gwynne Cars, Ltd was incorporated on 23 October 1925. It was a private company virtually wholly owned by Nevile Gwynne. The nominal capital was £3,000 in 2,000 Ordinary shares at £1 each and 20,000 Deferred shares at 1/- each. Of these Mr Gwynne took 1,000 Ordinary and 18,000 Deferred shares while the other two Directors, Mr C. V. Armitage and Mr A. E. de Burgh Jennings, took one Ordinary share each. Armitage had been works manager of Gwynnes Engineering and Jennings its company secretary. Mr Gwynne also took out a debenture for £12,000 on 25 November 1925 secured on all the property of the firm. As mortgagee he gave his London address as 16

Collingham Gardens, South Kensington, London. His permanent address, how-ever, was Deans, Piddinghoe, Newhaven, Sussex.

In the Return of Shares for the following year, there was a minor transfer of holdings from Mr Gwynne to the other two Directors. Mr Gwynne was described as Managing Director of William Foster & Co. Ltd of Lincoln though there is no record of his having been other than a Director. He was also described as a Director of A. G. Mumford & Co. Ltd. It is possible that this concern, which has not previously been mentioned in this history, was a predecessor of the firm of timber merchants which trades in Chiswick to this day. In the 1927 Return it was again confirmed that no invitation to subscribe for shares had been issued to the public. Gwynne Cars remained essentially a private concern.

On 20 December 1927, Gwynne Cars wrote to its agents to announce that finance for the next year was being satisfactorily arranged so that they could proceed with a programme of 300 cars for 1928. Surprisingly, given the small output of some five or six cars each week, it was around this time that C. M. C. Turner was engaged to design a new Gwynne 14/40 engine.

Gwynne Cars struggled on through 1928 but, at an Extraordinary General Meeting of the company on 18 October 1929, it was admitted that, by reason of its liabilities, it could not continue in business. It appointed a Liquidator to wind up the company voluntarily.

Towards the end of April 1930 the trade press announced that a sale by auction of the plant, machinery and stock of Gwynne Cars, Ltd would be held at Church Wharf on Tuesday 20 May. Wages continued to be paid to Frank Willment, works manager, until 7 December that year, however. Much of the plant and machinery was bought by Willment's family firm and was used by them for many years to maintain the equipment for their construction business.

The completion of the voluntary liquidation was reported to the Registrar of Joint Stock Companies on 17 June 1931. That completes the account of the financial aspects of the manufacture of Gwynne cars (the cars are dealt with in detail later on in the book). It is now time to return to the pumps side of Gwynne Engineering's activities. In 1925 when Gwynne Cars, Ltd was formed, that remained in the hands of the Receiver and Manager awaiting a purchaser.

Gwynnes Pumps, Ltd

Gwynnes Pumps, Ltd had no existence as a family firm save that Nevile Gwynne was a Director. It came into being as a wholly-owned subsidiary of William Foster & Co. Ltd. of Lincoln which took over the assets of the pumps side of the insolvent Gwynnes Engineering Company. This it did on 1 February 1927, completing the purchase by 13 April following. By the September of that year, some 2,000 tons of stock and machinery had been moved to the Firth Road site at Lincoln. The new company had a nominal share capital of £1,000 wholly owned by Fosters. In 1931 a sales and estimating office was built on the corner of Crisp Road and Chancellors Road opposite the site of the old Hammersmith Iron Works in London. This closed around 1965/66. At this point it is interesting to look briefly at the history of Fosters and the way in which it seemed to lead inevitably to the acquisition of Gwynne's pumps business. William Foster was born near Lincoln in 1806. After serving an apprenticeship in Manchester, probably as a millwright, he returned to Lincoln where, in 1846, he took over a flour mill on the River Witham at Waterside North. This he soon converted to steam. Around 1856, no doubt using general engineering skills learned during his apprenticeship, he abandoned milling and turned his premises into a foundry and workshop. Here he concentrated upon making agricultural machinery such as corn mills, thrashing machines and portable steam engines. By 1869 the export trade in such items was so successful that a branch works was opened in Budapest to serve the Balkans and, later, an office in Romania.

Foster was active in the social welfare aspects of local life and held many civic appointments including Alderman and Justice of the Peace. These culminated in his being made Lord Mayor of Lincoln in 1864. He died suddenly two years later at a time when none of his four children was involved in the business. When it was converted into a private limited liability company the following year, his partner William Frankish became Chairman and his nephew, Edward Foster Sandon, was made Managing Director. It was Sandon who had initiated the export trade to Eastern Europe.

43

Working capital was increased to £90,000 in the 1880s to finance expansion to meet the increasing demand for the company's products. The firm was still small compared to its major Lincolnshire competitors. These included Clayton & Shuttleworth of Lincoln (the patrimony of R. O. Shuttleworth the racing driver and of the Shuttleworth Collection at Old Warden Aerodrome at Biggleswade in Bedfordshire), Rustons of Lincoln and Marshalls of Gainsborough. It was Henry D. Marshall, the Managing Director of Marshalls, who interceded in the family dispute over Henry Gwynne's share of the J. & H. Gwynne partnership and again later to bring together the two competing Gwynne pump businesses.

As early as 1857, Thomas Aveling, the founder of Aveling & Porter of Rochester in Kent, pointed to the absurdity of using horses to haul the heavy 'portable' steam engines from field to field. From this developed the steam traction engine. Fosters were almost the last to enter this aspect. They did so in 1889, the year in which the firm became a public company.

In 1902 William Frankish was succeeded as Chairman by W. T. Page a Lincoln solicitor and Board member. In 1905, after Fosters had incurred heavy trading losses in Eastern Europe, Page interviewed William Tritton who had been engaged by Garretts of Leiston to liquidate its ill-founded German subsidiary when he was trying to sell some of its assets to Fosters. He so impressed Page that he was offered and accepted the post of General Manager.

William Ashbee Tritton was born in Islington in 1875, the son of a London stockbroker. He was educated at Christ's College, Finchley (which still survives) and King's College, London University. In 1891 he was apprenticed to J. & H. Gwynne where he so impressed that, during a strike, he was made shop foreman while still indentured. However, it is said that when John Gwynne deducted 4d. from his wages for tipping a porter, he resolved to leave Gwynnes as soon as he had completed his training.

After working at an assay company and as an inspector of steel rails, Tritton joined Thornycrofts at their Chiswick ship-building yard where he was responsible for making the circulating pumps for a new generation of Navy torpedo boats. The empty Thornycroft works was, of course, to be taken over by Gwynnes in the First World War for the manufacture of the Clerget rotary aeroplane engine. Before Tritton joined Fosters he was to gain further experience with the Metropolitan Electric Supply Company, and Linotype Ltd (the makers of hot metal type-casting machines for the printing industry).

In 1909 Fosters participated in the manufacture of what, given subsequent developments, was undoubtedly the most important steam traction engine of all the 900 or so that they made. Richard Hornsby & Sons, Ltd of Grantham had an order for a steam traction engine capable of hauling eight wagons the distance of 40 miles from Dawson City to Klondyke in USA. Supplies of coal and water were assured and, given the severe climatic conditions, steam propulsion was the obvious method. Hornsby's had stopped making steam engines and so they invited Tritton to cooperate in the project.

Hornsby's Managing Director, David Roberts, had filed patents for caterpillar tracks some years before and the publicity for this development had attracted the order. As no other orders materialised, however, Roberts had sold the patents in 1914 to Holts, an American tractor maker. Ironically, within a few months, the British government was placing orders with Holts to enable the Royal Naval Air Service to experiment with armoured tracked vehicles. That is where Tritton reappears.

Given Foster's reputation for quality and the experience that Tritton had gained on the Yukon project and on another for making petrol tractors to haul heavy guns for the Admiralty, they were ideally placed to make and test what became known as 'tanks'. Design work in conjunction with Lieutenant Walter G. Wilson R.N.V.R., a Cambridge mechanical sciences graduate, began on 2 August 1915, fabricating on 11 August and the machine first moved under the power of its Daimler sleeve-valve engine on 8 September. Tritton later modified the tracks and, after trials were complete, the first 100 tanks were ordered in February 1916.

After the war there were several claimants to the invention but the Royal Commission on Awards to Inventors decided that Tritton and Wilson were jointly responsible. Tritton was knighted and Wilson, by now a Major in the army, was appointed C.M.G. Wilson left the army when he was not promoted further. He formed Self Changing Gears, Ltd to exploit his further inventions and his epicyclic gearbox was adopted by both Daimler and Armstrong Siddeley cars and for many railway locomotives and railcars.

As a result of their successful wartime activities, Fosters were in a strong financial position when peace was restored. However, the export trade in agricultural machinery, which had comprised some seventy per cent of the business, had virtually disappeared and steam power had given way to the internal combustion engine. Moreover, responsibility for the design and manufacture of tanks had been concentrated at Vickers, Ltd and early makers such as Fosters had been eliminated. Thus, at the time when Gwynnes were in financial difficulty, Tritton was actively seeking to diversify his company's products. Given Gwynne's world wide reputation, his own knowledge of the firm and his experience on pumps, the purchase was a logical move. In addition it is clear from family sources that Tritton had a strong personal ambition to take over Gwynnes.

The main Board of Fosters was reconstituted to include Nevile Gwynne and C. V. Armitage from the original Gwynnes organisation as a condition of the takeover. The Board of the Gwynnes Pumps subsidiary comprised the main Board Chairman, Mr C. W. Pennell and Nevile Gwynne as Directors with Tritton as Chairman. There is no doubt that Mr Gwynne was a proud man and to have to serve as virtually a salaried staff member subordinate to his former apprentice must have been a bitter turn of events. It is hardly surprising that serious tensions arose from time to time.

The main aim of the new company and its Gwynne subsidiary was to design, manufacture and install pumping machinery for a wide range of purposes. In addition some agricultural machinery would continue to be made as would spare parts for existing products. Although the name of Fosters was good for credit, working capital was gradually increased to £500,000 by the 1950s. The sales side benefited from the Gwynne company's experience and its reputation for high quality in the pumps field.

Tritton replaced Pennell as Chairman of the main Board in 1939 but he resigned two years later due to ill-health and overwork after his designs for a new tank were rejected. He was replaced as Chairman of the main Board by Armitage and not, as might have been expected, by Nevile Gwynne. But Mr Gwynne was now 73 and, at 62, Armitage was the younger man. When Mr Gwynne retired from the two Boards is unknown, but as late as 1945 he still described himself in *Who's Who* as a Director of Fosters and Managing Director of Gwynnes Pumps. There is reason to believe that he still attended the London office on one or two days each week until shortly before his death in 1951.

Undoubtedly the acquisition of Gwynnes and the development of its products greatly helped Fosters to survive the passing of the steam age. Unlike so many of the eminent 19th Century agricultural engineering companies such as Aveling & Porter, Burrell, Clayton & Shuttleworth, Fowler, Garrett and Marshall, they achieved a smooth transition from the era of boiler-making to that of precision engineering in another field. Motive power was now provided for their pumps by oil engines and electric motors bought-in from other manufacturers although J. & H. Gwynne had developed oil engines as early as 1901.

Fosters were kept fully occupied on government contracts throughout the Second World War. A major activity was in the provision of fire pumps and trailer sets for the Auxiliary Fire Service in concert with the Standard Motor Co. Other important products were the suction dredgers which raised the hard core used in the construction of the Mulberry Harbours for the Normandy invasion.

When peace was restored they resumed their specialised work on pumps for land drainage, waterworks, sewage and so on. With the rebuilding of war-damaged cities and the building of new towns, the demand for the firm's products was considerable. The seemingly endless demand for power brought into being a new generation of larger power stations including nuclear stations at coastal sites. It was this factor which brought Fosters into close contact with Allens of Bedford.

The pumps specified by the Central Electricity Generating Board (C.E.G.B.) called for test facilities too large for either company to provide alone. The C.E.G.B's Chief Pump Engineer, L. O. Wild, yet another former Gwynne employee, insisted that this situation be remedied and so talks began between the two Managing Directors about the possibility of providing a joint test house. Mr Wauchope, who had joined Gwynnes in 1922 and Mr Norman Gwynne Allen were already well acquainted having been co-founders of the British Hydro-Mechanics Research Association. Norman Gwynne Allen was the grandson of William Henry Allen, former works manager of Gwynne & Co. and founder of the Bedford firm which bears his name. Clearly Gwynnes may well have disappeared as a separate entity but its influence was still all-pervading in the pumps world.

The talks appear to have reached no conclusion but, shortly after they ceased, Allens made a bid of £1.46m for Fosters. This was accepted and in September 1960 Sir Kenneth Allen, Chairman of Allens and son of the founder, became Chairman of Fosters. The merger was of immediate benefit to both companies. Allen's foundry had been closed since 1957 so that Foster's Wellington Foundry now met the casting requirements of both organisations. Allen's wide range of diesel and electric motors meant that the Foster side no longer had to buy power units for its pumps in the open market and the much needed large test house was built on the outskirts of Bedford.

In 1962 all pump manufacture was concentrated at the Wellington Foundry in Lincoln. The concurrent establishment of Allen Gwynnes Pumps, Ltd as a subsidiary of W. H. Allen, Sons & Co. Ltd meant the end of William Foster & Co. Ltd and its subsidiary Gwynnes Pumps, Ltd.

Allen Gwynnes Pumps, Ltd

Before looking at the history of Allen Gwynnes Pumps, Ltd it is interesting to reflect on the background of William Henry Allen and the Queen's Engineering Works of Bedford because, yet again as in the case of Fosters of Lincoln, it takes us back into Gwynne's own history.

William Henry Allen (1844-1926), the descendant of a well-to-do family from South Molton in Devon, was born in Cardiff where his father ran a prosperous catering business. After his father's early death William's mother Ann (1810-1887) continued the business. This, together with property she inherited at Barry, enabled her to participate with the Marquess of Bute in the development of Cardiff Docks. In particular she provided finance for the building of a new dock and new staithes for loading coal from rail to ship. On a personal note, it was at these docks that my maternal grandfather worked as foreman for many years.

At fifteen, William, who had been educated at Christ's College, Brecon, was apprenticed to a Llanelli foundry which made colliery machinery. The works was old-fashioned and everything had to be hand made. His apprenticeship completed, Allen returned to Cardiff to run, with his brother-in-law, a small foundry which his mother had purchased. The partnership was not a success and, in 1868, and now married, Allen decided to move to London. He applied to Merryweathers, the fire appliance makers, to a firm of marine engine manufacturers and to Gwynnes for a position.

In 1868, James Eglington Gwynne (1831-1915), who had taken over Gwynne & Co. founded by his father John I (1800-1855) decided to move from Essex Street to Brooke Street, Holborn. It was about the same time that his brothers John II (1838-1912) and Henry (1840-1889) decided to break away and start the rival Hammersmith firm. It was in these circumstances that Allen's approach to Gwynne & Co. proved most timely. Having originally replied that no vacancy existed, James wrote to Allen a few days later to ask for references. Thus, in 1869, Allen joined Gwynne & Co. in Brooke Street.

Years later Allen was to write:

> My future employer seemed to be impressed with my personality and after we had discussed the economics of workmanship he engaged me there and then, hardly allowing me to go home to fetch my bag. This part of my life was nothing short of romantic. I remained with Mr. Gwynne for eleven years and during the last few years the whole of the business was carried out by myself. I was not only the manager, but chief clerk, cashier, cost clerk, chief draughtsman, mathematician and general foreman of the whole establishment where we turned out £50,000 of work a year. My work there at the beginning was carried out under very difficult circumstances. The education I had had scarcely fitted me for that class of work and there was a great deal to be learnt. In two years, however, I gained the complete confidence of my employer.

That James appreciated Allen's worth was marked, if rather grudging-ly, when he presented him with a gold watch in 1877. The inscription read:

Presented to William Henry Allen
by J. E. A. Gwynne for his general ability.

Allen showed his respect for Gwynnes and the training he received there by naming his third son, who was born in 1874, Harold Gwynne Allen. This tribute was perpetuated in later generations.

When Allen joined Gwynnes the main business was in the manufac-ture of centrifugal pumps and the steam engines which provided the power. James Gwynne's interests were wide, however, and electricity generating sets were added later. These provided lighting for Billingsgate Fish Market and the Gaiety Theatre, for example. This broadened Allen's experience still further and, subsequently, with another employee whom he had engaged, the Austrian, Gisbert Kapp, he jointly patented methods of solving problems of voltage regulation, efficient slow-speed dynamo running and ventilation.

Increasingly James Gwynne left running the business to Allen while he travelled abroad seeking orders and spent time developing his own interests. This pattern was to be repeated later in his dealings with his son Nevile and with disastrous consequences. Inevitably Allen dealt direct with influential clients and eventually he was persuaded to set up on his own. This he did on 26 October 1880 by taking up a lease on rundown premises in York Street, Lambeth on a site which now forms part of Waterloo Station. A number of workmen from Gwynnes, where he had clearly been popular, followed him having marked the occasion by presenting him with a handsome clock inscribed:

Presented to W. H. Allen
as a mark of the esteem and regard
in which he was held by the employees of
Messrs. Gwynne & Co., Ltd. 26 October 1880.

One of the most influential contacts Allen made in his days at Gwynnes was with the Admiralty and, as he developed his interests in electrical machinery initially in the form of twin cylinder steam engines coupled direct to 12kW dynamos, he won orders for lighting equipment in Royal Navy ships and, subsequently, for merchant ships. Marine equipment was eventually to form the core business of W. H. Allen, Sons & Co. Ltd (as it was restyled in 1921) for many years to come.

By yet another coincidence, during the First World War, Allens, who in 1894 moved from York Road to a green field site in Bedford, were asked by the War Office to manufacture the Le Rhone rotary aeroplane engine. In all, the company made 3,221 engines at a cost of over £3m. Gwynnes' involvement in this field, in their case with the Clerget rotary, is described in a later chapter.

Like Gwynnes, after the war, Allens suffered from the loss of overseas markets, trade depression and labour unrest at home. Unlike Gwynnes, however, they prospered by concentrating on rebuilding their core businesses. Indeed they prospered to such an extent that, as we have seen, they eventually took over Fosters and, with it, its Gwynne Pumps subsidiary.

In the more recent reorganisation of January 1965, brought about by poor trading results in 1964, the separate trading subsidiary called Allen Gwynnes Pumps was absorbed into the parent company and so ended the story of the last organisation to include the name of 'Gwynne' in its title.

Subsequent Developments

Although not strictly part of the history of The House of Gwynne, it is of interest to look briefly at what happened after the name disappeared. Allens did not prosper. By 1966 the pumps business had declined further and press talk in the Autumn of the appointment of a liquidator showed the gravity of the situation. The electrical department was closed in the following year leaving diesel engines as the predominating element though some pumps were still made. Moreover, by 1968, under pressure of overseas competition, the ship-building industry of the United Kingdom had almost disappeared and with it demand for Allen's auxiliary marine equipment. Drastic action was obviously called for.

A merger of Allens with the long-established makers of compressors, Belliss & Morcom, Ltd of Birmingham was announced on 14 March 1968. This brought into being a new holding company called Amalgamated Power Engineering (APE), Ltd. The new group also included the separate Allen Gears of Pershore and the Belliss & Morcom subsidiary, Crossley Brothers Engines of Manchester, makers of the first internal combustion engine in this country and formerly of Crossley cars and buses.

The merger inevitably brought about a rationalisation of activities. One outcome was the transfer of the pumps side to Bedford and the closure of the Wellington foundry at Lincoln. With some 650 workers this was one of the biggest employers in that city and there was considerable civic and industrial unrest at the decision. Demonstrations, protest marches and pressure in Parliament, however, failed to stop the closure.

The 23-acre site was sold to Ruston-Bucyrus, Ltd, the company formed jointly by Ruston & Hornsby of Lincoln and Bucyrus-Erie of the USA to expand the mechanical excavator business. Plans to expand into tower cranes were, however, abandoned and the works were sold on to the GEC company Ruston Gas Turbines, Ltd (now ALSTOM Power UK, Ltd). To continue the string of coincidences in this narrative one of my sons, Nick, a chartered mechanical engineer, works for that company.

Allens continued to develop diesel engines, steam turbines and pumps but, with the expansion by the Ministry of Defence of its system of preferred suppliers, further rationalisation was inevitable.

The year 1977 saw the end of the Allen family connection with the firm that bore its name. This occurred with the retirement of Norman Gwynne Allen, CBE, Deputy Chairman of APE, Ltd. It also signalled the end of the Gwynne name in British industry.

In 1982, the share capital of APE, Ltd. was purchased by Northern Engineering Industries (NEI), Ltd. This Newcastle-upon-Tyne group includes several more household names in the engineering world including C. A. Parsons, the steam turbine manufacturers, the Reyrolle electrical equipment firm and International Combustion of Derby. Soon after this NEI, Ltd sold the designs of the APE pumps side, including those inherited from Allen Gwynnes Pumps, Ltd, to Weir Pumps, Ltd of Cathcart, Glasgow, the preferred suppliers of pumps.

Finally, in 1989, NEI, Ltd, including APE, Ltd, was acquired by Rolls-Royce plc to form part of Rolls-Royce Power Engineering, Ltd. The name of Allen survives in that the Queen's Engineering Works of Bedford trades as Allen Power Engineering, Ltd but the names of Foster and Gwynne are no more.

GWYNNE INDUSTRIAL HISTORY

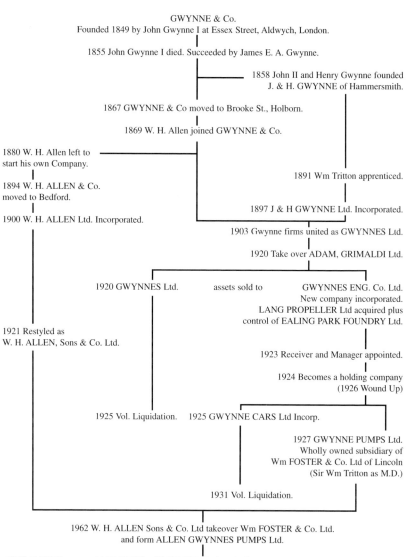

GWYNNE & Co.
Founded 1849 by John Gwynne I at Essex Street, Aldwych, London.

1855 John Gwynne I died. Succeeded by James E. A. Gwynne.

1858 John II and Henry Gwynne founded
J. & H. GWYNNE of Hammersmith.

1867 GWYNNE & Co moved to Brooke St., Holborn.

1869 W. H. Allen joined GWYNNE & Co.

1880 W. H. Allen left to
start his own Company.

1891 Wm Tritton apprenticed.

1894 W. H. ALLEN & Co.
moved to Bedford.

1897 J & H GWYNNE Ltd. Incorporated.

1900 W. H. ALLEN Ltd. Incorporated.

1903 Gwynne firms united as GWYNNES Ltd.

1920 Take over ADAM, GRIMALDI Ltd.

1920 GWYNNES Ltd.   assets sold to   GWYNNES ENG. Co. Ltd.
New company incorporated.
LANG PROPELLER Ltd acquired plus
control of EALING PARK FOUNDRY Ltd.

1921 Restyled as
W. H. ALLEN, Sons & Co. Ltd.

1923 Receiver and Manager appointed.

1924 Becomes a holding company
(1926 Wound Up)

1925 Vol. Liquidation.   1925 GWYNNE CARS Ltd Incorp.

1927 GWYNNE PUMPS Ltd.
Wholly owned subsidiary of
Wm FOSTER & Co. Ltd of Lincoln
(Sir Wm Tritton as M.D.)

1931 Vol. Liquidation.

1962 W. H. ALLEN Sons & Co. Ltd takeover Wm FOSTER & Co. Ltd.
and form ALLEN GWYNNES PUMPS Ltd.

1968 ALLENS merge with BELLISS and MORCOM Ltd. and others to form AMALGAMATED POWER
ENGINEERING (A.P.E.) Ltd.
Transfer of ALLEN GWYNNES PUMPS Ltd from Lincoln to Bedford.

1977 A.P.E. Ltd acquired by NORTHERN ENGINEERING INDUSTRIES Ltd.
Pumps business sold later to WEIR GROUP of Glasgow.

1989 N.E.I. acquired by ROLLS-ROYCE POWER ENGINEERING p.l.c.

54

Chapter Three

The Pumps

THE MANUFACTURE of pumps was their core business and, as matters developed, there is ample reason to regret that the Gwynnes did not confine their activities to that area. Instead they allowed themselves to be seduced by the mirage of fame and fortune into making motor cars which, in the inter-war years, was to be the ruin of many old established engineering concerns. It is not without significance that there is a direct link from Gwynnes through Fosters of Lincoln and Allens of Bedford to Weirs of Glasgow who manufacture large pumps to this day.

A brief consideration of the design of the centrifugal pump follows prior to looking at the expansion of its uses by Gwynnes into many other fields than its original application. That was to raise water with the obvious corollary of replacing windmills and scoop wheels by more efficient methods of draining and reclaiming water-logged land such as that found in the fen districts of East Anglia.

Fundamentally the centrifugal or velocity pump functions by inducing a flow of water the speed of which is increased as it passes from entry to exit. The speed at exit is determined by the diameter and speed of the impeller. The liquid discharged from the impeller is replaced by fresh liquid forced up the suction pipe by atmospheric pressure. Thus a continuous flow is created as opposed to the intermittent flow which is characteristic of the reciprocating pump.

At first all Gwynne pumps were driven by steam engines of their own design but, around the turn of the century, far more efficient oil and electric motors began to replace steam as prime movers. As early as 1901 Gwynnes brought out their own four-cycle range of oil engines. These were offered in sizes from 2.5 to 25 hp in single cylinder form and in 32, 40 and 50 hp sizes in twin cylinder form. However, in the extensive fen drainage installations equipped with Gwynne pumps, other makes of oil engine were also bought in including Blackstone, Crossley, Petters and Ruston.

Two 30-inch Gwynne Pumps driven by Ruston Oil Engines at the Old Pump House, Fiskerton, Lincolnshire. Total capacity of 150 tons at 12ft 6in. head. Installed September 1861.

In all forms of velocity pump, the size of the pump and the speed of the impeller are determined by several variables. These include the diameter of the impeller, the area and angle of its blades and the volume of water and the height to which it has to be raised. As the speed of the impeller was increased by the introduction of ever more powerful prime movers, so the design and size of pumps changed radically.

The other factor affecting design is the direction of the flow of water. In the standard centrifugal pump, water is discharged at right angles to the direction of its entry to the impeller whereas in the mixed flow pump its course is changed by about 45 degrees. In the axial flow pump the water is discharged in the same direction as it enters. Basically the axial type is capable of passing greater flows while the straightforward pump, although it has a lower throughput, is capable of raising the flow to greater heights.

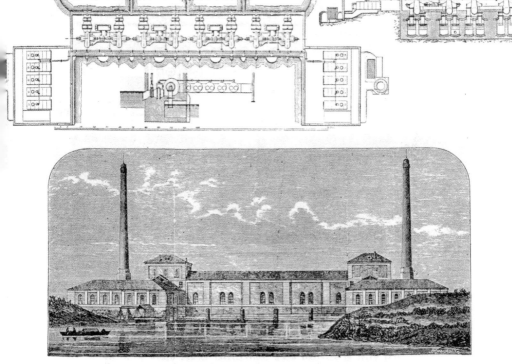

A world famous installation. The Ferrara Pumping Station in Italy, 1873. Eight Gwynne Pumps discharged over 2000 tons a minute in the reclamation of the Ferrara Marshes.
Reproduced from the publication *100 Years of Gwynne Pumps* (publication No. 783), published by the Directors of Gwynne Pumps Ltd in 1948.

The Gwynnes Pumps 102 inch Invincible Pump still produced after the takeover by Foster Wheelers of Lincoln. Reproduced by kind permission of the Hammersmith and Fulham Archives.

In the centrifugal pump's basic use for land drainage Gwynnes secured numerous contracts world-wide. Apart from some ninety sets installed in East Anglia, the firm's first major plant overseas was built at Ferrara, Italy as early as 1873. This was to deal with an area of 127,000 acres at the Adriatic outlet of the River Po. The plant comprised four compound Gwynne condensing steam engines driving eight centrifugal pumps to deliver 2,000 tons of water to a maximum lift of 12 feet. Further orders followed in Italy and then in Holland, France, Egypt, Guyana, etc. and the firm prospered.

During the First World War the firm continued with its traditional work. After the war, however, the deterioration in labour relations and general trade depression, coupled with the failure of the car side, meant that Gwynnes were removed from control by the family and absorbed into the Lincoln company of Fosters. It prospered under its new management. In the traditional field of land drainage Gwynnes secured contracts world-wide and its products ranged from small domestic sets to the three massive 102-inch diameter pumps installed at St. Germans, Kings Lynn. Each of these has a capacity of 1,000 tons of water per minute and at the time were the largest pumps ever made in Britain. Interestingly a Gwynnes' catalogue has a photograph of a Morris Minor saloon car occupying about one-half of the diameter of one of these pipes. One could wish that it had been a Gwynne Eight car.

Gwynnes Engineering Co. Ltd of Hammersmith advertising their range of Centrifugal Pumps soon after the First World War.
Reproduced by kind permission of the Hammersmith and Fulham Archives.

In 1933 the new King George V Graving Dock was opened at Southampton. Designed to take the largest Transatlantic liners then known of up to 60,000 tons displacement, the Dock held 57 million gallons of water which had to be pumped out in four hours. Gwynnes were responsible not only for the design and manufacture of the pumps but also for the installation of all the machinery and equipment including the four 1,250 hp motors.

The simplicity of the basic construction of the centrifugal pump soon led to the development of its uses into other areas such as the movement of sewage, sludge, acids, tar, gravel and, in unchokeable versions, even very large solids such as stones and rocks. Pumps made of porcelain, by contrast, were made for use with fine chemicals where the elimination of all risk of metallic contamination was essential. With time further uses came about such as dredging, refrigeration, ventilation and irrigation in all of which Gwynnes were to the fore. Indeed, in an article in the Lincolnshire Magazine, C. V. Armitage, the company Chairman, pointed out that the range of varieties and sizes of pumps produced by the company numbered nearly one thousand.

During the Second World War, still under the control of Fosters, Gwynnes Pumps, Ltd manufactured over 17,000 pumps of all sizes and types including a large number for floating and graving docks. Most of the aggregate for the construction of the Mulberry Harbour and for airfield runways was lifted by Gwynne-built dredgers and their attendant barges for receiving the spoil. More than fifty land drainage pumping stations were provided with the firm's pumps to increase food production. Hundreds of foam pumps were provided for airfield crash tenders and numerous portable pumping sets were delivered to the Armed Forces for water supply. The manufacture of fire-fighting equipment will be dealt with in a separate chapter.

After the war, more than half the firm's products were sold overseas in twenty-eight different countries. At home the rebuilding of bomb-damaged towns and cities and the development of new satellite towns led to considerable demand for pumps for use in storm water, sewage and water supply installations. The advent of the new larger power stations called for bigger centrifugal pumps to provide the increased volume of cooling water. These in turn created a requirement for larger testing facilities than the existing companies could finance and so brought about the series of amalgamations and take-overs that eventually led to the demise of Fosters and its Gwynne subsidiary.

The immediate result of the take-over and the establishment of Allen Gwynnes Pumps was a sizeable increase in production. In addition, the expertise of Allens in the manufacture of diesel engines and electric motors enabled all pumps to be produced with their own integral prime movers. Thus the pumps could be tested as a complete unit.

At the Biddenham Research Laboratory and Test House the electrical power was provided by an Allen diesel-alternator set. Here large, medium and low head pumps with both horizontal and vertical suction branches could be tested. Three measuring legs each contained a venturi-meter designed to cope with a combined flow of 150,000 gallons per minute. Suction conditions could be varied for minus 20 to plus 20 feet and the pipe-work permitted working up to a 200 feet head.

The firm continued to produce centrifugal, mixed and axial flow pumps for marine applications, for waterworks, land drainage, irrigation, docks, power stations, sewage works and other industrial applications.

Small electric-driven pump at the Bass Museum showing the diversification of Gwynnes.

The Wellington Foundry at Lincoln listed over 50 graving and impounding dock contracts and more than 150 waterworks, sewage and land drainage installations. In addition pumps for special duties were developed such as for ash disposal at power stations, sand, gravel and dredging pumps. Even complete dredgers were built at Lincoln and launched into the River Witham.

Unhappily, things began to go wrong once more. British ship-building declined and eventually the pump designs and drawings were sold to the Weir group and by 1968 the name of Gwynne finally disappeared from the trading market.

Chapter Four

The Aeroplane Engines

The Background pre-First World War

Given the contribution made by British aircraft to the successful out-come of the Second World War, it may be difficult to appreciate that, at the outbreak of the First World War, there was little by way of a serious aircraft industry in Britain. Indeed, as late as 1911, the only British aircraft engine to power an aeroplane which completed the Circuit of Britain was one designed by Gustavus Green.

Between 1910 and the outbreak of war, however, aviation in the country was encouraged by the offer of a number of prizes put up by both individuals and companies. For example in the first trial, sponsored by one P. A. Alexander, to find a British engine capable of running for 24 hours and giving an output of 35 bhp, only the Green engine out of six entrants ran for the stipulated time; even so it pro-duced insufficient power to win the award. Both the Humber and Wolseley examples failed the test.

A second Alexander trial was held at Farnborough the following year. Of seven manufacturers who entered, only Green and E.N.V. actually presented engines for test. The Green 60/65 bhp engine com-pleted the two twelve-hour runs non-stop and recorded 61.6 bhp at 1,150 rpm. This performance, together with success in other tests, won the company the prize.

In 1914, the Naval and Military Aero Engine Competition was held at Farnborough. Out of 26 engines submitted, 13 were withdrawn before the tests started. Eight of the remainder performed successfully, but again the Green engine won, this time with a six-cylinder 100 bhp version. The other successful engines included an Argyll sleeve-valve, an Austro-Daimler design built by Beardmore, a Salmson water-cooled radial, a Gnome rotary from France and entries by Anzani, Sunbeam, and Wolseley.

Despite his success in these competitions, however, Green's designs, all of which were sub-contracted for manufacture mainly to Aster Engineering of Wembley, London, saw little aviation use in the war. This was because the Government decided as a matter of policy that reliability had to be sacrificed for lightness in military aeroplanes. As early as 1910 tests of over 70 different types of engine had been carried out. These differed in configuration from vertically placed cylinders through horizontal, V and radial to the rotary design. The tests had shown that power-to-weight ratios had ranged from 7.0 lbs per bhp for vertical-cylinder engines to 2.8 for the rotary. Most of the other types of engine were liquid-cooled but even the similarly air-cooled radial versions, of which twelve makes were tested, were almost twice as heavy per bhp as the rotary.

In France, however, a different perspective prevailed. As early as 1908, the three Seguin brothers of Paris had developed the original idea of Felix Millet to produce the seven-cylinder Gnome engine specifically for aviation requirements. This became necessary because the standard car-type, in-line, water-cooled engine was proving too heavy for its power output. Additionally air-cooled motor-cycle patterns such as the J.A.P. and the Anzani lacked the power and were incapable of continuous full power running without overheating. In these circumstances, the Gnome rotary (giving 50 bhp without overheating for a weight of less than 150 lbs) was ideal and did more to help develop early flying than any other make or type of engine.

The Seguins achieved these results by concentrating on the use of the new nickel steel alloys of very fine section. For example, the cylinder walls of the Gnome engine were no more than 1.5 mm thick. This meant that a favourable power-to-weight ratio could be achieved compared to that of a conventional in-line engine.

The Position at the Outbreak of War

By 1914, two other French firms were building their own versions of rotary engines. These were Clerget-Blin of Levallois-Perret, an industrial suburb north-west of Paris and Le Rhone also in Paris. They were founded in 1911 and 1912 respectively. Clerget rotaries conformed more closely to normal engine practice than the other two in that they had two separately operated valves per cylinder. Le Rhone used a single push-pull rod and Gnomes had only a single valve (the Mono-

Clerget 7Z Rotary Engine manufactured by Gwynnes during the First World War.

soupape) to pass exhaust gases out and allow some air to enter the cylinder to weaken the over-rich mixture entering through transfer ports in the two-stroke manner. Although Gnome took Le Rhone over in 1915, the two factories continued to produce distinct types of engine throughout the war in which together they made over 20,000 units.

Thus it was to France that the Admiralty, which was responsible for the Royal Naval Air Service (RNAS), and the War Office, responsible for the Royal Flying Corps (RFC), had to look for tried and tested aero engines which would conform to the policy laid down and which could be imported or manufactured under licence. Licences granted to British companies provided most of our requirements. Gwynnes made the Clerget, Allens of Bedford the Le Rhone and Hookers of Walthamstow the Gnome. Gwynnes also granted a licence to Ruston, Proctor of Lincoln, an agricultural machinery company who, unlike Gwynnes, went on to make complete aeroplanes.

Interestingly, Germany produced rotary engines either through pre-war licensing arrangements or by copying captured Le Rhone engines. In addition they also imported engines from the Swedish manu-facturer Thulinmotor who made Le Rhones under licence. Rotaries therefore powered the main combat aeroplanes of both sides.

The Role of Gwynnes

The need for urgent wartime expansion of both the RNAS and the RFC (the two did not combine to form the Royal Air Force until 1918) meant that established and reliable engineering companies had to be found who would undertake the task of manufacturing the existing proven French aircraft engines under licence. Both Gwynnes and Allens had done work for the Admiralty over many years and were obvious candidates for such contracts.

Thus it came about that, around December 1914, the Air Department of the Admiralty approached Gwynnes to make the new 100 bhp Clerget-Blin rotary. At first, Gwynnes demurred but, with the promise of an exclusive licence and of financial backing, they agreed. As there was no room at Hammersmith, they found new premises in the old Thornycroft shipyards at Church Wharf, Chiswick, London. These had been used for the construction of torpedo-boats and destroyers until those vessels had grown too large to be launched so far upstream. Initially Gwynnes took over one quarter of the works from the British Motor Cab Co., the rest being let to small engineering companies. But an immediate order from Vickers for 100 engines for the War Office and an increase by the Admiralty in its original order from 50 units to 1,000 before any had been delivered caused the Government to commandeer the whole works. Advances of capital enabled Gwynnes to renovate the buildings, install electric power, purchase the necessary plant and machinery and to select and train the workforce. Several members of staff, including Mr C. V. Armitage and Mr Henry Humphreys (both of whom were later to become directors), were sent to France to study the technical aspects of the design and its fabrication.

The adoption of the Clerget rather than the Gnome was due to the recognition by the Government that the 50 bhp Gnome would be too under-powered for the developing use of aircraft from the original reconnaissance work and that of spotting for artillery to the more exacting tasks of fighting and bombing. Thus the Clerget was developed from the early seven cylinder Type 7Z of 80 bhp. *Jane's Fighting Aircraft of World War I* [1] and Gwynne's own catalogue show that development of rotaries took place over the war years as follows:

Type	7Z	9Z	9B	9BF	9J	11EB	BR2
Cylinder	7	9	9	9	9	11	9
Bore (mm)	120	120	120	120	105	120	140
Stroke (mm)	150	160	160	172	140	190	180
Compression	4:1	4:1	4:1	5.3:1	5:1	5.1:1	5.2:1
Ave. rpm	1200	1180	1250	1250	1300	1300	1300
Nominal bhp	80	110	130	140	——	200	——
Effective bhp	85	115	135	146	100	230	230
Wt per bhp (lbs)	2.75	3.45	——	2.56	2.50	2.21	2.16

We know that W. O. Bentley was drafted to Gwynnes as a naval engineer officer for a time and the effect of his proposals is looked at later. He persuaded the firm to introduce aluminium pistons and uprate the 110 bhp Type 9Z to 130 bhp Type 9B. Gwynnes themselves later

---

1 *Jane's Fighting Aircraft of World War I*, Studio Editions Ltd., 1990, Engines Section Part B; compiled from *All the World's Aircraft* published yearly during the First World War.

brought in the 140 bhp Type 9BF by increasing the crankshaft throw by an almost unnoticeable 6.1 mm thereby increasing the stroke to 172 mm and, in turn, raising the compression ratio. No other part was altered. Gwynne's catalogue shows that they also made some of the 16 bhp horizontally-opposed twin-cylinder Clerget engines but it is not known to what purposes those were put.

Clerget 9B Rotary Engine manufactured by Gwynnes during the First World War.

One engine which does appear in the catalogue, perhaps surprisingly given the outcome of the Bentley episode, described further on, is the BR2. The BR1 does not appear so we must assume that the firm was eventually ordered by the Admiralty to make the BR2 in view of its better performance. The BR1 is thought to have been made by Humber and Vickers only.

Gwynne Clergets were used in several different makes of British aeroplane, the most notable being the famous Sopwith Camel (130 bhp Type 9B). Other Sopwith aircraft powered by Clergets included the Triplane, the Baby, the 11/2 Strutter and the Snipe.

The Fairy Hamble Baby Seaplane was another. The Avro 504K training biplane used Gnome and Le Rhone engines as well as the Clerget 130 bhp. Other fighters which used Clerget rotaries included the Bristol Scout 'Bullet' and the Vickers FB19 both of which were fitted with the 110 bhp Type 9Z.

Most surprisingly there is no record in *Jane's* of any French aeroplane using the Clerget in the war though a note seen in the Shuttleworth Collection does suggest that some Nieuport aeroplanes used Ruston, Proctor-built Clergets.

Technical Aspects of the Clerget Design

In looking more closely at the technical aspects of the Clerget design, we are greatly indebted to the late Tony Carlisle who, having rebuilt to flying standards a French-made Clerget Type 9BF of 140 bhp for the RAF Museum at Hendon, London, wrote an article about rotaries for an early Gwynne Newsletter.

Carlisle was later asked to examine a Gwynne-Clerget. His comparison is of interest. Of the French engine made by Delaunay-Belleville he explained that it was polished almost like watch parts with a coating of castor oil which afforded excellent rust protection. Colour was added to this beautiful work by copper plating on rockers exposed to exhaust gas and by nickel-plating on induction pipes. By contrast, the Gwynne had a rather poor 'as-turned' finish and blued induction pipes more as one would expect from a wartime munitions contract.

The principle of the rotary engine is that fuel and air are drawn in through a hollow stationary crankshaft emerging into the crankcase between the crank webs. The mixture passes around the big end assembly and connecting rods to manifolds which convey it to the combustion chambers. This long and tortuous induction route was eventually to tell against improvement of power output other than by increasing the swept volume which, in turn, merely served to exacerbate the 'breathing' problems.

But that problem was for the future. At the outbreak of the First World War the rotary operating in a normal four-stroke cycle, with its odd number of cylinders arranged in one plane around the crankcase like the spokes of a wheel, offered good mechanical balance, equally spaced firing intervals and good cooling without the need for heavy liquid coolants. In particular it was the lightest form of piston aero-engine for any given capacity. This favourable power-to-weight ratio over all other types of engine was vital for powering the flimsy fight-er aeroplanes of the time.

The engine differed from the radial type, which it superficially resembled, in that the propeller was fixed to a rotating crankcase, whereas in the radial the propeller was mounted on the crankshaft in the conventional manner.

The engine worked by drawing air through the hollow crankshaft (58 mm internal diameter in the Clerget) and mixing it with a jet of petrol from a pressurised tank at about 2 psi. There was no choke on the car-burettor but two control levers, one for air and one for petrol, left the pilot to compute the mixture for all conditions of height, speed and so on. Rotaries were made to run at full power. The 20% reduction in power which was possible without rough running was sufficient to enable a formation of aircraft to keep station.

When descending, petrol was cut off entirely but, for approach and landing when power might be wanted quickly, an ignition earthing button (known as the 'blip switch') was fitted to the control column. As the engine was, in effect, a large flywheel it could be kept turning slowly with occasional bursts of power.

The fact that almost the whole engine weighing some 300 lbs revolved at 1,250 rpm did raise questions about balance. However, parts were machined from high grade forged steel to a standard weight and this proved adequate. The manual prescribed balance within 30 grammes but conceded that engines containing many spare parts could be more than twice this margin out of balance. In practice the Clerget was perfectly smooth running and incomparably better than, say, a Tiger Moth Gipsy engine or a small radial.

Each cylinder in a rotary fired as it passed the vertical and, having nine cylinders, two or three were on power strokes at any moment. The firing order was 1-3-5-7-9-2-4-6-8. Twin magnetos were affixed upside down on the stationary mounting drum. They delivered up to 6,000 sparks per minute each via a large multiple slip ring used as a distributor from which bare piano wires radiated to eighteen sparking plugs.

Unlike the cylinders on the Le Rhone engine which could be readily removed, Clerget cylinders were clamped between the two halves of the forged crankcase and were not normally removable. They were turned from high-grade steel with thin finning and a wall thickness of only 2.5 mm. Gnome cylinders were even thinner at 1.5 mm and Le Rhones had cast iron liners in the steel cylinder barrels. Cylinder heads were in one with the cylinders having milled finning varied slightly to give accurate balance. Valve rockers were not only of identical weight for rotary balance but had hammer head balance weights to counteract the centrifugal force arising from push rods and tappets.

Valve operation was one of the most interesting and unusual parts of the engine. Each valve train, inlet and exhaust, had a sixteen-toothed wheel fixed off-centre to mesh with a ring which had eighteen internal teeth and which revolved with the crankcase. The off-centre mountings of the sixteen-toothed wheels were stationary on the crankshaft extension. Thus, on each revolution the off-centre wheel was advanced by two teeth or one-ninth of the revolution relative to the engine. However, every fourth tooth was advanced laterally to become a cam for valve operation on each alternative revolution as required by a four-stroke engine. All gear teeth and cams were semi-circular in profile and the cams did not brush past the tappets but rolled up to them and away. Some profiling was obtained by shaping the tappet faces. Surprisingly, the French Clerget engines built by Gwynne and Ruston, Proctor all had slightly different valve timing.

Inevitably all Clergets suffered from uneven cooling, the leading side of each cylinder being cooled more than the trailing side as they rotated. Thus distortion occurred putting the cylinder bore out of round and causing high spots which, if the piston did not seize, showed up blue from the outside and had to be hand-lapped during the service routine. To try to maintain compression in a distorted cylinder, a special obdurator piston ring was used in the top position. It was, in fact, a double thickness ring made of thin silver/copper alloy and of 'L' section so as to reach up to the piston crown. The theory was that gas pressure inside the ring flange would force it to take up the distortion of the cylinder wall. This temporarily overcame the problem but the life of the obdurator ring was no more than 25 hours running and a more permanent solution had to be found.

At one time engines were giving a life in action of about fifteen hours before seizing. This brought about a heavy loss of trained air-crew and aircraft and so the noted engineer, W. O. Bentley, was commissioned into the Navy expressly to find a solution.

It is interesting to read Bentley's comments in his autobiography about his reception at the Chiswick factory:

> ...Nevile Gwynne, the good-looking chairman, appeared to welcome me. I gathered that he was a man who had to be treated circumspectly... Armitage, the works manager, was an easier proposition... In spite of the position of authority I occupied, I was soon neck-deep in the politics, manoeuvrings and jealousies that arise when an outsider is let into the design department... I managed to persuade Gwynnes to raise the compression ratio and, because they were ordered to do so, they accepted the aluminium piston, but I met a series of carefully contrived obstructions when I tried to... incorporate aluminium cylinders with cast iron liners to provide conductivity...which would equalise the temperature... But at this stage I think that Gwynnes thought they were being led into an entirely new design which would mean dropping the Clerget. Besides they were also occupied with a new rotary of their own for which they had brought over a designer from France.

The outcome of his frustration was that Bentley asked the Admiralty to remove him from Chiswick. He was posted to the Humber works in Coventry where he must have been welcomed as a breath of fresh air after that firm's interminable task of producing hundreds of bicycles. It was at Humber that Bentley developed the Admiralty rotary AR1 which became known as the BR1. This produced 150 bhp and was followed by the BR2 of 230 bhp. Both engines could be seen to follow the accepted general arrangement for rotaries which owed much to the Clerget design.

More recent evidence in a book by David G. Styles entitled *Rileys and the Kaiser War* suggests that the disagreement between Gwynnes and Bentley may not have been just a matter of pique but that there may have been a fundamental difference in engineering principles. The Riley Engine Co. together with the Nero Engine Co. of Foleshill made a range of components which were supplied to Gwynnes and to Ruston, Proctor for Clerget engine assembly. This included alloy pistons for the Clerget 9B.

When 208 Squadron was re-equipped it was provided with Sopwith Camels powered by 130 bhp Clerget engines in place of its previous BR1s. Those engines, unlike the Clergets, had very narrow section, delicate piston rings which had a tendency to break even on assembly let alone in the air. The Squadron Commander later reported that, while Clerget Camels were slightly slower and had a nominally lower power ceiling, they were much more reliable than their Bentley-powered predecessors. This was confirmed by the Engineering Supplies Officer who put the difference down to a lower engine speed and higher torque. Could it be that, while Nevile Gwynne agreed to introduce the aluminium piston, he insisted on staying with the design he knew and the suppliers he could trust? We shall probably never know but the comments in this book do throw an interesting new light on a well-known incident.

To conclude Carlisle's account, this metric-designed rotary ran entirely on ball bearings of Imperial measurement. Lubrication was by a total loss system using castor oil. This remarkable oil, which even today stands up better than mineral oil under extreme conditions, was delivered by a complicated plunger pump at the rate of 1.5 gallons per hour. It did not readily mix with petrol in the crankcase and, in spite of cowlings intended more to contain oil flung out than for streamlining, it saturated the crew's clothing and the rear of the fuselage. It is interesting to note, incidentally, that the 'R' of Castrol 'R' stands not for 'Racing' as is widely believed but for 'Rotary'.

According to *Jane's*, the engines from Clerget Type 9Z onwards have the advantage of greater accessibility in that all the working parts are easily removable from the front without having to disconnect the engine from the airframe. Carlisle did not, however, find matters so straightforward on the old engine No.52757 that he dismantled. This 17.5 litre Gwynne 9BF did not respond to the normal stripping routine. When eventually he was able to withdraw the pistons and examine an engine which had almost certainly not been touched since the end of the war, he found that the carbon deposit was exceptionally heavy. One cylinder, if not two, showed the signs of the blueing which preceded seizure. In all probability the engine had started the ominous clanking which was the warning of imminent trouble. At least it had been withdrawn from service before another casualty had occurred.

Gwynne's Production Figures

There is some doubt about the number of Clerget engines produced by Gwynnes. The Chairman's report at the Ordinary General Meeting of Gwynnes Ltd on 20 January 1920 claimed that "...something like 3,600 engines..." were made. The formal record is in Volume III of *War in the Air* [the official history], which shows Gwynne's production as:

80 bhp Type 7Z
100 ordered of which 42 were delivered in 1916 and 5 in 1917.
The balance of 53 was cancelled or suspended.
110 bhp Type 9Z and 140 bhp Type 9BF
1,750 ordered and delivered between September 1915 and July 1918.

There is no mention of the 130 bhp Type 9B. We know that the company made that version not only because it was the outcome of W. O. Bentley's intervention but also because a surviving example in a private Essex collection has been examined. This bears Gwynnes' makers plate bearing the serial number 14060.

Gwynnes held an exclusive licence from the Admiralty which gave them the sole British manufacturing rights to the Clerget. At an early stage they granted a sub-licence to Ruston, Proctor Ltd, the Lincoln manufacturer of agricultural machinery. Rustons, who also made complete aeroplanes, notably the Sopwith Camel, produced:

110 bhp Type 9Z and 130 bhp Type 9B:
1,300 between 1916 and 1918.
140 bhp Type 9BF: 600 in 1918.

The most likely explanation of the apparent discrepancy between the official figure and that quoted by the Chairman of Gwynnes is that he included Ruston's 1,900 engines thereby bringing the total number of Clergets manufactured under Gwynnes' licence to 3,697.

As pointed out earlier, Gwynnes did not make any BR1 rotaries. According to one source, however, they did receive an Admiralty order for 1,000 BR2s near the end of the war. Of these only 82 were delivered in November 1918 before the order was cancelled. Other makers of the BR2 were Daimler, the main contractor, with 1,415, Rustons with 596, Humber 391 and Crossley 83. Gwynnes also, in 1918, delivered eleven of the twelve 170 bhp ABC Wasp engines ordered.

Interestingly, Gwynnes still showed four Clerget engines of nine and eleven cylinders at the Olympia Aero Show of 1920. It was not until May 1924, however, that they reported the disposal of some of the stock of aviation engines and spares.

Rotaries after the First World War
Almost overnight after the war the pre-eminence of the rotary engine as a form of aerial motive power disappeared to be replaced by fixed in-line or radial designs. Various reasons have been advanced for this. They include:

- limitation of speed due to centrifugal stress;
- power loss due to windage of rotating cylinders;
- gyroscopic effect on the aircraft especially in turns;
- high fuel and oil consumption; and,
- need for frequent overhaul and exacting standards of workmanship.

The last point is particularly true in that, by 1918, fixed water-cooled in-line engines could run for 100 hours between overhauls compared to about 20 for rotaries.

Nevertheless the main factor was that, with the end of fighting, the power-to-weight ratio became less important than the potential for development. There is no doubt that, largely because of the complexity of its induction process, the rotary was restricted by ceilings to its output imposed by its inherent design constraints. The output could be raised by increasing the swept volume but that merely increased the 'breathing' difficulties. On in-line engines, by contrast, the inlet process is simple and direct.

In wartime conditions such drawbacks could be tolerated when alternative power units were heavy and so imposed a performance penalty on combat aircraft. Once war ended, however, and research could be resumed, the limitations of rotaries could be seen and development was transferred to more efficient types of engine. Significantly, even the inventive M. Clerget turned to radials and to experimenting with diesel aero engines until, in the 1920s, he sold out to SNECMA.

Rotaries continued to be used in military aircraft for a few years; for example, an RAF squadron of Sopwith Snipes was sent to Iraq as late as 1926. However, the availability of cheap, redundant military aeroplanes did pander to the desire of wartime pilots to continue flying and brought about the travelling air-circus. This provided a daring display of aerobatics as well as offering many people their first experience of flying at 5/- (25p) for a short trip. Even here, however, it was not the Clerget that was favoured but the Le Rhone. This was largely because its individual cylinders could be easily removed for the frequent cleaning and valve grinding that was needed. All was to end in 1935, however, when the Air Ministry refused further Certificates of Airworthiness for rotary-engined aircraft.

This eclipse of the rotary after the First World War was mirrored almost exactly after the Second World War by the replacement of the piston-engine by the turbo-prop and then the jet in high-performance aircraft.

In the address by Nevile Gwynne, to which I have already referred, he bemoaned the fact that the rapid spread of civil and military aviation he had anticipated had not come about. The Government, he said, had deserted the industry. But, even if the aircraft industry had prospered, it is now evident that it would not have been on the basis of the type of engine that his firm had made and developed so successfully.

Surviving Gwynne Clerget Engines

A few rotary engines survive, mostly as museum exhibits in either public or private hands. It has not been possible to establish how many of these are specifically Gwynne made (indeed, some are unidentifiable). Therefore listed are all the rotaries that have been found.

The Clerget which was indisputably by Gwynnes is a beautifully restored example in a private collection at Billericay in Essex. It bears a maker's plate inscribed:

Clerget-Blin Motor No.14060, Type 9B.
Manufactured by GWYNNES Ltd.,
Engineers, London. Licensees for the British Empire.

Two Clergets are fitted to aircraft in the Brooklands Museum at Weybridge, Surrey. The Avro 504 training biplane has a 110 bhp Type 9Z made by Ruston, Proctor Ltd. This is No. R.1214. The second aeroplane is a Sopwith Camel fit for ground running only. It is powered by a 130 bhp Type 9B. This, No. 5113, was made by Automobiles Delaunay-Belleville of St. Denis, Seine, France.

The Clerget rebuilt by Tony Carlisle, No. 52757, is a Type 9BF of 140 bhp, Gwynne-built. It is owned by the Shuttleworth Trust of Old Warden, Biggleswade, Beds. After its return, parts of the engine were used to keep the Trust's Sopwith Triplane flying regularly. Its original engine, No. 4/1729 39328A, was made by Moteur d'Aviation SDGD of France. The rest of engine No. 52757 is now being restored in Germany to an airworthy state. On completion this will be fitted to a replica Sopwith Camel, the air frame for which is being constructed for the Trust by Northern Aircraft Workshops of Dewsbury, West Yorkshire.

The Trust has a third Clerget but much of the information about this has been polished out of the maker's nameplate. It is either a 9B or a 9Z made by Ruston, Proctor, Ltd which has been sectioned for demonstration. The number 7260 appears on No. 1 cylinder.

The RAF Museum at Hendon admits to several Clergets but neither the Museum itself nor its Restoration Centre at Cardington, Beds. can give full details partly because the engines in several cases are installed in aircraft slung from the ceilings of large hangers. In particular the names of the manufacturers are not recorded. A Type 9B, No.2622/34946, is in store at Cardington whilst another 9B is at Hendon. This is the Delaunay-Belleville which was restored to flying condition by Tony Carlisle. It is fitted to a Sopwith 1^1/$_2$ Strutter on display.

The Fleet Air Arm Museum at Yeovil has a Sopwith Baby and a Camel both fitted with rotary engines. That in the Baby is a Clerget Type 9Z of 110 bhp of unknown origin. The Camel engine was made by Ruston, Proctor but no more is known.

The rotary engine in the Museum of Lincolnshire Life at Burton Road, Lincoln, is something of a mystery. It is thought to have been brought to Lincoln when Gwynnes moved up from Hammersmith and to have been fitted to a Sopwith Snipe of 1917. The Ruston archivist suggested it was possibly a surviving Gwynne-Clerget but the only legend which it bears is 'Coventry type PLR. Patent No.C.7517.' According to *Jane's* the Snipe was fitted with the 200 bhp Bentley BR2 though other sources do refer to Snipes having been equipped with Clergets. The two Coventry-based makers of the BR2 were Daimler and Humber. The patent C.7517 was taken out by one J. Price of Co. Cork in 1912 and relates to screw propellers. The entry in the Patent Office also refers to W. O. Bentley in concert with Dawson & Co. Ltd all of which points to the engine being not a Clerget but a BR2. The propeller fitted to it is stamped '110 hp No. 2726. Diameter 274 mm. Pitch 2120. LP710C'. This could mean that it was made by Lang Propellers, Ltd for a 110 bhp Type 9Z Clerget. On balance we think that, while the Museum may have a Gwynne-BR2 or Ruston, Proctor-BR2, we think it more likely that it was made in Coventry and that, for display only, the aircraft was fitted with a propeller from a Type 9Z Gwynne-Clerget.

The only other Clerget known at the time of writing is the one restored by Mr Laurie Fletcher of Allestree, Derby, for his private collection. Some of the parts came from an Avro 504K which crashed into the River Humber in 1917. They were brought up in the nets of a trawler as late as 1992. Other parts were obtained on an exchange basis from the Shuttleworth Collection and Mr Fletcher fabricated the remainder himself to bring the engine to 90% completion. Not surprisingly no indication of its origins survived its long immersion.

That sums up the known UK population of Clergets. As to other makes of rotary, the Shuttleworth Trust has two Bentleys both made by Humber and both sectioned for display. The BR1 of 150 bhp is No. 433. The BR2 was made in November 1917 and is marked No. 1. There is no information about Gnome or Le Rhone survivors and none was mentioned to us in our research. No doubt examples exist on display in France as do other Clerget survivors.

The History of Other Rotary Makers

Although concerned essentially with the story of Gwynnes, it is interesting to complete the picture by glancing briefly at the subsequent histories of the other makers of rotaries whom we have mentioned. Those of Bentley, Daimler and Humber are too well-known to merit repetition here. Gwynne's immediate associates, Ruston, Proctor of Lincoln amalgamated with Richard Hornsby & Sons Ltd of Grantham in September 1918 to form Ruston & Hornsby Ltd. Like Gwynnes, they set out on the motor car manufacturing path with the high quality Ruston-Hornsby car. The natural trend towards the mass-production of cheaper cars brought this venture to an end in 1924. Rustons went on to make Ruston-Bucyrus mechanical excavators and later were taken over first by English Electric and subsequently by GEC. As makers of gas turbines they still survive under the umbrella of ALSTOM Power UK, Ltd.

In France, where Gnome had taken over Le Rhone in 1915, the combined Gnome et Rhone concern also attempted to make a high-class 40 hp six cylinder car but gave up after only four had been produced to concentrate on motor-cycles. At first they made the British Bradshaw and ABC under licence but, from 1923 onwards, they produced their own conventional single-cylinder machines with which they had many competition successes. In the late 1920s they also introduced BMW-like flat twins in pressed steel frames. After the Second World War Gnome et Rhone concentrated on small two-stroke machines until they ceased production in 1959.

Thus, of all the names mentioned in this chapter on aeroplane engines, only that of Bentley survives and that in an almost un-recognisable form in foreign hands.

Chapter Five

The Albert Cars

WHEN, AT the end of the First World War, there was no call to continue to make aeroplane engines, Gwynnes were left with a fully-equipped specialised factory and a workforce trained in engine manufacture. In the words of the Chairman at the General Meeting of Gwynnes, Ltd in January 1921: "...clearly the only thing the plant was suitable for was to adapt and to start manufacturing motor car engines". It is perhaps significant, in the light of their subsequent histories, that W. H. Allens of Bedford in a similar position did not take the same road, but returned to prosperity by making those products which had been their core business before the war. These comprised centrifugal pumps, diesel engines, electric motors and fans.

On 1 November 1919 there appeared the following announcement in the trade magazine *Motor Commerce*:

HELP WANTED IN CAR PRODUCTION
The manufacturers of a well-known light car, having works in the London district, ask us to invite manufacturers who have the facilities to do so to assist them in securing a large production. The demand for their car is really extraordinarily encouraging and it will not be possible to meet it unless help is forthcoming. What is wanted is a manufacturing concern in or near London with large

premises and plant capacity that would be suitable for the production of light cars either in part or in whole. If the proposal interests anyone we shall be glad to forward letters in confidence if addressed to Box 118 at this office.

The Albert – a promotional photograph

An illustration of 'The Albert Car' on a deck of playing cards.

Could this have been the siren call which lured Gwynnes on to the rocks? We know from the report of the liquidation of Adam, Grimaldi & Co. Ltd that it was towards the end of 1919 that Gwynnes, Ltd entered into an agreement to supply engines for the Albert car so this could well have been the case. Certainly the outline descriptions of both advertiser and victim could well fit the bill.

The firm of Adam, Grimaldi & Co. Ltd was first registered on 19 December 1917 as a company to produce aircraft parts. After the war it turned to motor car assembly with the Albert car. The name was taken from the Albert Embankment off which its factory was sited. As far as we know, Mr Grimaldi's experience of the motor business was largely on the sales side. Mr Adam had previously worked with the noted Scottish engineer Alex Govan on the design and production of the Argyll car.

It is a well-known fact of automobile history that, after a promising start, Argyll's ambition outran prudence and that they built a grandiose and lavish new factory at Alexandria-by-Glasgow. *The Autocar* commented at the time that the plumbing arrangements alone probably cost more than some competitors had spent on a complete factory. The combination of two such partners as the sales-driven Grimaldi with Adam from such an extravagant background hardly suggested an efficient, well-run, down-to-earth operation. Be that as it may, this was the company with which Gwynnes became involved.

The car which Adam, Grimaldi proposed to market emerged as the 12 hp Albert. In its issue of 7 December 1918 *The Autocar* magazine contained a brief announcement that this would be manufactured on a quantity basis almost entirely at the firm's own works. British throughout, the engine was to be of four cylinders with bore and stroke of 68 mm and 103 mm (1,494 cc) and overhead valves. A single plate Ferodo clutch would transmit the power to a four-speed gearbox and final drive would be by enclosed propeller shaft, with a disc-type universal joint to a helical-bevel driven rear axle. It was hoped that, with full equipment, the car would sell at about £300.

The Albert was designed by A. O. Lord. In his *Complete Encyclopaedia of Motor Cars*, Georgano remarks that "...cars designed by Lord tended to be dogged by misfortune"; this was to prove only too accurate. *The Vintage Motor Car Pocketbook*, though not Georgano, said that it originally used a Dorman side-valve engine. An Albert car so powered was once owned by Alexander Coaches of Sheffield, but this must have been a one-off because a search of the Dorman engine records for the years 1918-20 has failed to reveal any bought by Adam, Grimaldi. Two were supplied to Gwynnes but these were later sold on to a firm in Redhill, Surrey.

From time to time during 1919, *The Autocar* published details of the Albert and other new cars in the form of a buyers' reference guide. Some of the changes made to its specification suggest that there may have been teething troubles, particularly with the transmission. For example, by April 1919 the Ferodo clutch had given way to a fabric disc clutch and that, in turn, by the November had been replaced by the familiar leather-faced cone. This could indicate that the Ferodo clutch was causing problems with the back axle or with the half-shafts and that a less fierce solution had to be found. It was not surprising, therefore, to find that an Albert driven by E. G. Grimaldi, which was entered for the June 1919 London to Edinburgh Trial, was one of six which failed to start.

The Albert Model G1 of 1920

In the event the car was launched at the Motor Show in November 1919 for the 1920 season. It was marketed as a light car de luxe though Georgano dubs it as:

> ...one of a crop of worthy, unremarkable light cars that appeared after World War I to cater for the boom in popular motoring.

The usual eulogies in the motoring press spoke of:

> ...the display of the Albert cars...already caused some sensation on account of the reputation of this manufacturing firm...a high class car at a reasonable price...vast crowds surrounded the stand...the many excellent features of the chassis on view were greatly appreciated.

The Albert

MEETING THE UNPRECEDENTED DEMAND FOR THIS LEADER OF LIGHT CARS DE LUXE

The 12 h.p. Albert is taking the road in ever increasing numbers week by week. Touring, 2-seater, Coupe and Saloon Models are pouring forth from the highly organised works of Gwynnes Engineering Co., Ltd., of Chiswick, and the unprecedented demand for this leader of Light Cars *de luxe* is in a fair way to being satisfied. "The Alberts are coming." And with the Albert car, as its life partner,

A Service which means more than a Guarantee.

The Albert is based on the principle of continuous satisfaction being ensured to every owner. A chain of Service Depots is being established at suitable points throughout the country. These Depots are manned by specially-trained mechanics who will help and advise Albert owners as to the running and tuning of Albert Cars. Their interest in every Albert Car is maintained throughout its life.

THE 12 H.P. ALBERT IS MANUFACTURED BY GWYNNES ENGINEERING CO. LTD ,OF CHISWICK, OF CLERGET ROTARY AERO ENGINE FAME

SOLE CONCESSIONNAIRES: THE SERVICE MOTOR CO., LTD,, 245, OXFORD STREET, LONDON, W.1.

Advertisement from The Autocar *July 1920 for The Albert, manufactured by Gwynnes Engineering Co. Ltd, of Chiswick.*

In fact, Lord's design was that of a totally conventional car whose only unusual features were a four-speed gearbox and large, spacious bodywork in aluminium. The four-cylinder engine was monobloc with detachable cylinder head. It had a bore of 68 mm and a stroke of 103 mm giving a capacity of 1,494 cc (not the 1,496 cc so often quoted) and an output of 26 bhp at 2,200 rpm. The pushrod operated overhead valves had rockers that were pressure lubricated. The pistons, following Gwynnes' revised practice with the Clerget aero-engines, were of aluminium alloy. Water cooling by thermo-siphon eliminated the need for a pump. Transmission was by leather-cone clutch, three universal joints fitted with Hardy-Spicer flexible disc couplings and Carden shaft to a helical bevel back axle. Suspension at the front was by quarter-elliptic springs while at the rear a cantilever system was adopted whereby the rear end of each spring was designed to slide on a pad which, in turn, was free to move on the axle casing.

An important feature not revealed by this written specification had been clear since the first technical drawings appeared in *The Autocar* on 7 December 1918. This was that:

> ...two large plain bearings secure the massive crankshaft, thus reducing machining...and the tail bearing is of greater size to take its greater load.

This was hardly an encouraging message for intending customers.

Though *The Autocar* continued to refer to 'helical toothed pinion' in the rear axle, if *Fletcher's Index* is to be believed that was replaced by a straight bevel by the time of the 1919 Motor Show. Indeed, of the 191 models on display at that event, 56% had straight bevel rear axles, 24% helical while the rest comprised worm, chain, spur and belt. This suggests that there were no spiral bevel examples though the magazine does seem to have used the terms helical and spiral synonymously at that time.

The company had appointed The Service Motor Co. Ltd, then of 245 Oxford Street, London, W1 as sole concessionaires and they had obtained in Stand No. 109 at Olympia, a prime site in the centre of the front row opposite the main entrance. The Service Motor Co. was a new enterprise formed expressly to market the Albert through the agency of recognised motor dealers supported by service depots established countrywide. In announcing the enterprise in Motor Commerce in August 1919, Mr George Mitcheson, the Managing Director, said that the intention was to produce the car at the rate of 3,000 in the first twelve months from December 1919, increasing annually up to an output of 10,000 per annum. How this was to be achieved from the cramped Albert works was not explained. The Service organisation later moved to premises at 94 Great Portland Street, London.

Strangely no prices were quoted in the pre-Show guide published in *The Autocar.* Nor were any given in advertisements even as late as 27 December of that year. However, the prices given in *Motor Commerce* on 15 November 1919 showed £469 7s. 6d. for the chassis, £534 10s. 0d. for the two-seater, £539 10s. 0d. for the tourer, £665 10s. 0d. for the closed coupé and £826 5s. 0d. for the saloon – a far cry from the £300 estimated in Adam, Grimaldi's first announcement. Nevertheless these prices attracted sufficient attention for 3,000 firm orders to be taken with deposits placed to a total value of £1.7m. The prices in-cluded two spare wheels with tyres and one year's free insurance.

The disastrous effect of the strike of foundry moulders, which started in October 1919, just before the Motor Show, is reflected in the fact that the chassis numbers given for this model in *Stone & Cox's* price guide run from 110 to 350 only. This gives a production total even lower than that in Nevile Gwynne's subsequent statement that the firm had met only about one-eighth of the 3,000 firm orders. In fact it was not until June 1920 that Gwynnes were able to deliver completed cars and then only in small numbers.

As we have seen, Gwynnes came into the picture when Adam, Grimaldi failed to pay for the first batch of rolling chassis delivered. As Gwynnes were to find when they took the defaulters over, the premises were far too small to match Adam, Grimaldi's expansive programme of mass production. Extensive and costly reorganisation was needed before efficient production could begin. One would have thought that one visit would have shown this to be the case and that the briefest examination of accounts at Companies House would have revealed the gross under-capitalisation. However, as we have learned from published works about the family, the male Gwynnes were an irascible lot. So it could well be that, even if Nevile Gwynne's financial and technical advisers had counselled caution, they would have been overruled. The outcome was that when Adam, Grimaldi defaulted, Gwynnes took over the manufacture of the complete Albert car at Chiswick, the Albert works being confined to body production.

By 7 August 1920, the effect of the industrial action had so disrupted production that, although it had been formally settled six months before, of the cars ordered and for which deposits had been taken, the greater part of 1,500 were held in stock awaiting engines. As a result, on the advice of the concessionaires, Gwynnes agreed to return to each agent one-half of the deposit standing to his credit on the books.

Moreover, because the price of bodywork had virtually doubled, savings brought about by the more efficient production of chassis were more than offset. Accordingly the prices of complete cars had to be increased. Even so, by adjusting their estimated profit, Gwynnes claimed that they had kept the cars more than competitive in price. In fact this claim was somewhat optimistic. The 11.9 hp Morris Oxford, admittedly with a side-valve engine and three-speed gearbox, was available at £385 for the two-seater and £495 for the tourer while the Morris Cowley was even cheaper. The Albert did, however, cost slightly less than the 11 hp Riley.

Nor was all well with the finished car technically since one owner later reported that, after having his front springs replaced and the chassis members strengthened to eliminate whip, he had eventually had his original body fitted to a new model G2 chassis which was a great improvement.

The Albert Model G2 of 1921

Though the November 1920 Motor Show reports suggested that few changes had been made to the existing model G1, the wheelbase had been increased from 9ft 1in. to 9ft 6in. and the gear ratios had been changed to 4.5:1, 6.5:1, 12.75:1 and 18.0:1. However, conflicting reports in different issues of *The Autocar* seemed to suggest that suspension and transmission changes were being made. On 30 October 1920, in its *Buyers' Guide*, the magazine referred to quarter-elliptic springs at the front and half-elliptic at the rear, whilst in later issues, the original cantilever arrangement at the rear was prescribed. As to the transmission, both straight and helical bevel rear axles were recorded. In fact, over the Show as a whole there had been a radical change in the pattern of rear axles. Whereas in the previous year straight cut bevels had predominated, this year the newly-introduced spiral bevel was to be found in 53 per cent of models while the straight cut had been reduced from 56 per cent to 27 per cent of rear axles. *The Autocar* commented that the new cut was far quieter in running though it had been a troublesome task to manufacture. This deficiency was being overcome as new tools were introduced and workers became more skilled. The magazine then compounded the confusion by referring to the spiral bevel axle as having helically cut teeth.

The Albert G2 Model. Courtesy of Tony Graven in Manchester.

As to performance, *The Autocar* found on 14 May 1921 that, with four people up, the car climbed Brooklands Test Hill at 10 mph and covered the mile at 40 mph both from a standing start. Other reports claimed a maximum speed of a little over 50 mph. Petrol consumption was said to be 30 mpg though one reader claimed to average no more than 22 mpg in hilly Cornwall and another averaged 27 mpg.

In April 1921, competition forced Gwynnes to reduce the selling prices of their cars by an average of £100 varying with the model. Thus the price of the complete tourer was reduced to £495 but only one spare wheel was provided and the offer of one year's free insurance was withdrawn. Even so, the Morris Oxford tourer cost £446.

On the question of competing in motoring events for publicity, the company set its sights against speed competitions. As Mr Gwynne was to say at a meeting of his shareholders on 4 November 1921:

> ...we know that the conditions of such tests do not satisfy the owner who prefers to see standard cars, such as he can buy in the ordinary way, successfully come out of reliability tests for endurance and hill-climbing, tests which the owner may at any time call on his car to go through.

As early as May 1921 an Albert four-seater driven by C. H. Chandler was entered in the London to Edinburgh Trial organised by the Motor Cycling Club. The press reported that Chandler made a very impressive climb of Butterkiss Pass in Wensleydale, the summit of which is 1,726 ft above sea level. Chandler was awarded one of 56 Gold Medals out of 100 starters. The following July, two Alberts were among fourteen starters and won one Gold and one Silver Medal in a Trial organised by the Light Car Club in the Bournemouth area. These successes were recorded with the G.2 model which was shortly to be superseded.

The Albert Model G3 of 1922

The first advertisement for the new G3 appeared in *The Autocar* of 17 September 1921. In introducing the car for the November 1921 Motor Show, the press referred to a number of improvements. These included semi-elliptic front springs in place of the quarter-elliptics together with general strengthening of the chassis and its extension at the front to accommodate the new springs; a new sliding-gate gear-change and further minor changes to the gear ratios; a fabric-faced single plate clutch in place of the leather covered inverted cone; and new stub axles and steering assembly with larger ball joints and bearings to give a better steering lock.

90

At some stage, too, the engine was inclined to bring the transmission into a straight line from flywheel to back axle whilst, on the cosmetic side, a new radiator with sloping sides was fitted.

The question of the type of transmission used was finally resolved on the acquisition of a copy of the *Owners' Handbook and Catalogue of Spare Parts* for the G3 model. This made clear that the Albert still used a straight bevel rear axle until its replacement by a spiral crown and pinion from chassis No. 1,350 onwards.

On 4 November 1921, Mr Gwynne's Report to shareholders at the Ordinary General Meeting included a historical survey of events since the firm entered the car business. In it he spoke of:

...the introduction of this model having involved the discarding of finished parts to a very considerable value...the only wise and proper policy to follow...in view of the competition and of the imperative necessity of keeping up the standard of our car.

There is no doubt that substantial losses were incurred by the changes needed to make the car more reliable but it was not clear from the context to which model change Mr Gwynne was referring on that occasion.

The prices of the car in *The Motor* magazine shortly before the Motor Show were £425 for the chassis, £495 for an open two- or four-seater, £640 for a closed coupé and £665 for a full 'All-Weather' body. A special Service All-Weather model was offered at £525. At the same time, however, a Morris Cowley open four-seater cost £376, a Bean £395 and a Morris Oxford £446 5s. 0d. Moreover at the 1921 Show some fourteen cars costing less than £400 were exhibited. These included such well-known names as Jowett 7 hp, Lagonda 11 hp, Singer 10 hp and Standard 8 hp. In addition Buick, Dodge, Horstman, Peugeot, Swift and Wolseley among others all showed models costing less than the Albert so that, despite favourable comments on its performance, comfort and ease of maintenance, competition was severe. It was not surprising, therefore, to find that by 9 March 1922 the prices of the various Albert models had been reduced to £350, £440 and £448, £555 and £560 respectively and the Service All-Weather to £475.

On the road the car showed a comfortable cruising speed of 35 mph and a maximum of a full 50. Average petrol consumption was 28 mpg. Once again the flexibility of the engine and its ability to pull away from 5 mph in top gear were remarked upon favourably.

In competitions the G3 model was showing up well in 1922. In two early outings commendable finishes in tough long-distance trials went unrewarded because inexperienced entrants infringed the rules by, in one case, turning up early at a stage and, in the other, by failing to have the requisite number of passengers aboard. In April a particularly severe London to Land's End Trial saw even such redoubtable contestants as Kaye Don and S. C. H. Davis penalised for stopping in unauthorised places on Porlock. S. C. Westall's Silver Medal rewarded an excellent performance in such conditions given that only 16 out of 82 starters won Gold and that he had bought the car only a few days before the Trial.

By June, *The Autocar* carried an advertisement to the effect that Albert cars had completed a 1,000 mile road trial, made 100 climbs of the Brooklands Test Hill and run for 24 hours all non-stop and all under RAC supervision. In the 24-hour run the first 12 hours were spent on the Brooklands track and the remainder on public roads.

Later the same month came the first appearance of a driver who was to be associated successfully with Alberts and, subsequently, Gwynnes for several years. This was C. W. D. (David) Chinery, a London motor-dealer with premises opposite the Olympia arena in Hammersmith. He won a Gold Medal, as did Westall, in the London to Manchester Trial. In October, Chinery led four Alberts in the Southampton to Exeter Trial all of which completed the event. One of the other drivers was J. F. Deverill who was later to join the staff of Gwynnes in charge of sales and who, like Chinery, was to become one of their most successful competition drivers.

It would seem that the Albert was, at last achieving reliability. However, Gwynnes Engineering themselves were not prospering and, on 21 July 1923, a Receiver and Manager was appointed. One of his first actions was to drop the Albert marque altogether. He gave as his reason the fact that: "...the first 11.9 Albert car was weak in design and gave the vehicle a bad name which was never really lived down".

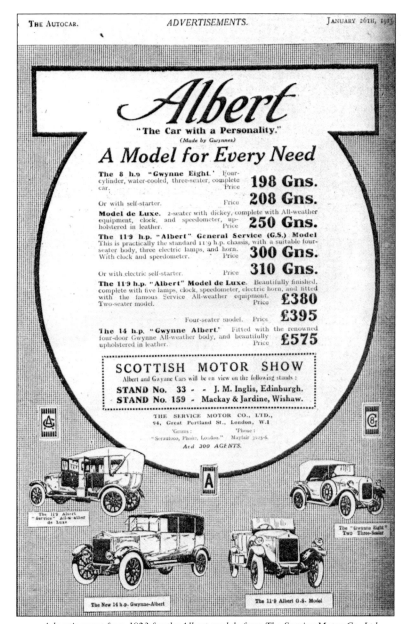

Advertisement from 1923 for the Albert models from The Service Motor Co. Ltd of Great Portland Street. Advertised in *The Autocar.*

No doubt this view is reflected in the comment by T. R. Nicholson in his book *The Vintage Car, 1919–1930* (Batsford, 1966) where he says: "A weak rear axle plagued this car" (page 285).

The contrast between the conclusion reached by the Receiver – a Chartered Accountant and a layman in engineering terms – and the eulogy delivered by Mr Gwynne to shareholders in the preceding January is most marked. Mr Gwynne then recorded that:

> ...the reputation gained by the Albert car in 1921 has been maintained in every way and the 1922 model continued to gain the highest distinction in all competitions and tests and generally afforded universal satisfaction.

As to the number of Alberts made, the chassis numbers suggest that, in addition to the 900 of models G1 and G2, some 650 of the G3 were made from chassis No. 1,350 to the highest number recorded. In addition, of course, some early models were made before the transmission change. In all it is probable that some 1,600 Albert cars were made.

There are seven survivors on the Register in this country and one early car which has not been traced and probably exists only in rumour. In addition there is one 1920 Albert in Australia. One of the British cars was the subject of an article in the magazine of the Aluminium Development Council in 1956. The Council was impressed by the condition of its bodywork after years of exposure to the elements and particularly by the state of its bonnet which, as was the Albert practice, had never been painted. Other aluminium parts which were found to be in excellent order were the crankcase, valve gear cover, sump, gearbox and the pistons.

The All-Weather Head

This equipment, the precursor of the modern convertible bodywork, first appeared as a Gwynne product in a coachbuilding trade journal of July 1921. Later that year, Messrs. George and Jobling of Newcastle-upon-Tyne showed two examples at the Motor Show, one of which was on a Wolseley chassis.

An improvement on earlier attempts, which suffered from a tendency to rattle and which proved difficult to stow, the Gwynne head was designed by Mr G. H. Wenham of Messrs James Young & Co. Ltd of Bromley, Kent, the well-known coachbuilding firm. Wenham had joined the firm as early as 1910 and was still with them in 1935 by which time he was Works Director.

He applied for a patent on 31 March 1920 on the basis that his design was an improvement on earlier versions. Patent No. GB 168349 was granted on 31 August 1921. The purchase of the patent by Gwynnes Engineering was announced by the Chairman at the General Meeting of 21 January 1921 which does suggest that it was made conditional upon the eventual grant. The sole manufacturing rights were granted to G. Beaton & Son (1919) Ltd of St. James's Square, Holland Park, London. Over the years the head was known variously as the Albert, Gwynne, Service or Portland All-Weather Equipment and the Beatonson Head.

Early versions were based on the then almost universal touring body with its folding hood and celluloid side screens but these soon evolved into the ultimate fully glazed four-door saloon type. It was the need to deal with the extra size and weight of this last version that brought about the introduction of the 13.9 hp Gwynne-Albert at the 1922 Motor Show.

The All-Weather Equipment appears to have sold well because examples were used by coachbuilders as far apart as Eastbourne, London, Northampton, Reading and Yeovil and on chassis as diverse as AC, Fiat, Ford, Rolls-Royce, Rover, Sunbeam and Vauxhall in addition to Gwynne's domestic use. A Beatonson example appeared as late as the 1929 Motor Show.

The 14 hp Gwynne-Albert

Despite the general trade depression and the dire financial position of the firm itself, which by 1922 had an overall deficit of £478,545, this was the point at which Gwynnes chose to incur the expense of introducing two new models, the larger of which was designed '...to meet public demand for a car of greater power to seat five'. The other model was the Gwynne Eight with which will be dealt with separately later.

In general layout the new car closely followed the original Albert.

The Gwynne Albert. Courtesy of Lincoln Library.

The engine was, however, redesigned and increased in size to 75 mm bore and 110 mm stroke to give a capacity of 1,944 cc and a Treasury rating of 13.9 hp. To meet the increased power it was based on a three-bearing crankshaft. The wheelbase remained at 9ft 6in. but the track was increased to 4ft 6in. An Autovac, which drew the fuel supply from a tank at the rear, replaced the earlier gravity feed system. Cooling was by thermo-siphon in standard Gwynne practice.

Once again on test the smoothness of the engine and its ability to pull away in top gear from walking pace was emphasized. Acceleration was a marked feature and by stop-watch 30 mph was reached from a stand-

96

ing start in just under 13 seconds. The best gait of the car was found to be about 40 mph when there was not the slightest vibration. The suspension over bumpy roads was also commended whilst in indirect gears there was a total absence of hum from the transmission.

At its introduction the Fourteen was priced at £480 for the tourer and £575 for the All-Weather. It was uncompetitive from the outset, however, as the Morris Oxford with its 13.9 hp engine cost £95 less as a basic tourer.

The sole surviving Gwynne-Albert 14, XN-5267, is kept in splendid condition in Northern Ireland. This was the car described by Michael Worthington-Williams in the March 1986 issue of *The Automobile* magazine.

A 1923 Gwynne-Albert All Weather Body.
Originally restored in 1986 and acquired in 1992 by its current owner, Raymond Moffatt
[pictured], who maintains it in its immaculate condition.

There is no information about the number of Gwynne-Alberts produced between the model's introduction and its scrapping along with the Albert by the Receiver.

So ends the story of the ill-fated Albert marque.

Chapter Six

The Gwynne Cars

FOLLOWING THE decision of the Receiver, Gwynnes concentrated on two models, the Fourteen and the small Eight.

The Gwynne Fourteen

Apart from such minor matters as the replacement of the Gwynne-Albert's Claudel-Hobson carburettor by a variable jet SU and the provision of side lamps on the front mudguards, the only important change in the specification of the Fourteen from that of its predecessor appears to have been an increase in the wheelbase from 9ft 6in. to 9ft 10in. Otherwise it retained the 75 mm x 110 mm push-rod operated overhead valve four-cylinder engine of 1,944 cc.

The car was described in a road test by *The Motor* as "…an ideal vehicle for the owner-driver of moderate means". On the road it proved capable of 58 mph with a full load but the outstanding feature was the way it could be driven at 35 to 40 mph for mile after mile without any sign of stress. Indeed at 40 mph the engine was quite silent. Petrol consumption averaged 28 mpg whilst oil consumption was negligible.

When it was introduced in October 1923 the standard touring model cost £450 though by the following year this had been reduced slightly to £410. A four wheel brake version was available for £25 extra. Once again favourable comment was made on its capacity for high average speed without fuss, its excellent suspension and cornering ability and upon the full equipment provided.

The Fourteen was to continue to be manufactured until about March 1928 when it no longer appeared on the firm's price list. Originally it was described as the 14/30. Surprisingly, given the continuing financial weakness of the company, around 1927 C. M. C. Turner, who had driven Gwynne Eights in competition (and most notably in the Junior Car Club's 200-mile races at Brooklands in 1926 and 1927), was engaged by the firm to design a new 14/40 engine of the same 1,944 cc capacity to produce 30 bhp at 2,000 rpm.

The car was available as a tourer, saloon and a most attractive sports model. This last provided accommodation for three adults on the front seat and one in a dickey seat in the pointed tail. The sports was the first Gwynne to adopt wire wheels in place of the customary artillery type. They made a significant improvement to the appearance of the car and cause one to wonder why the company did not use them exclusively.

By 1927, the price of the Fourteen was set at £285 for the tourer and £475 for the saloon and remained so throughout the year. The saloon was provided with four–wheel brakes as was the sports car. That cost £495 and clearly must have had superior performance to that of the standard models though, unfortunately, test figures for it do not appear to be available. Nor do the company publicity brochures give any performance data though 80 mph is mentioned in some articles.

There is little information about the number of 1,944 cc cars of various types manufactured. *Fletcher's Index* shows the chassis numbers starting at 0100 in 1923; the surviving Gwynne-Albert first registered on 18 April of that year is No. 0115; the 1924 series started at No. 0148. This suggests an output of 48 cars in the first year. Turner spoke of an output by 1928 of "…no more than three in the last batch". If we assume a steady fall in demand each year then we are probably looking at a total output of no more than 200 Fourteens, including Gwynne-Alberts. This makes all the more surprising the decision by Nevile Gwynne to incur the costs of designing and tooling up for a new engine so late in the car's life. Maybe it is yet another example of the irrational decision-making which seemed to bedevil the Gwynne firms.

100

No Gwynne Fourteens as such survive in UK. There are two in Australia.

The Gwynne Eight

This was by far Gwynne's most successful model. It was first mentioned in the motoring press in October 1922. Mr Gwynne referred to it in the Annual Report of Gwynnes Engineering Co. Ltd of January 1923. Clearly the company was hoping that, like Austin, it would be saved by introducing a successful small car for the masses.

The Eight's Antecedent – the Spanish Victoria

The reference made by Mr Gwynne in his Annual Report to testing on the Continent and persistent rumours of a Spanish origin necessitated communication with vintage car organisations in that country. These approaches brought a response from Dr Miguel Elizalde Biada, the youngest son of the late Arturo Elizalde, the noted car and aero-engine designer. Dr Elizalde confirmed that the Victoria car, designed by the Technical Department of the Elizalde automobile factory in Barcelona under the supervision of his brother, Salvador, was the origin of the

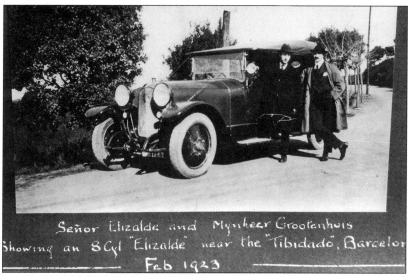

The 1923 8-cylinder Elizalde, said to be the forerunner of the Gwynne Eight.
Reproduced by kind permission of the Hammersmith and Fulham Archives and Dr Ing Miguel Elizalde Biada.

Gwynne Eight. This led to an introduction to the owner of the only known surviving Victoria, Don Fernando Redondo Berdugo of Madrid from who supplied details of the car. The car is now maintained perfectly by Don Fernando's son.

It seems that the incentive for the small Victoria to be built by a firm noted for its large luxury cars was a market survey carried out by Arturo Elizalde. This convinced him of the need, post-First World War, for a small car of simple design powered by a sturdy four-cylinder engine. The original outline specification still survives in the archives of the Fundacion Elizalde and Dr Miguel has kindly provided us a copy:

A small car of excellent performance to enable two people to go about their business at minimal cost. It should have a small four-cylinder engine powerful enough for it to go anywhere and be provided with a self-starter within the closed all-weather type of bodywork. It could have either three or four road wheels and, because it will have a small engine and be of light weight its transmission could be via continuous gear changes and only one driving wheel. An oil lamp will suffice for town driving with acetylene for the road.

With a few important exceptions the specification for the Gwynne Eight was identical to that of the Victoria. This is so despite the fact that Gwynnes claimed that it had been substantially redesigned at Chiswick. The main differences lie in the transmission. While both had three-speed gearboxes, where the Victoria had a single dry-plate clutch with drive by universal joint and Carden shaft to the left rear wheel only, the Gwynne has a leather-lined inverted cone clutch and final drive by spiral bevel with a torque tube and orthodox differential. Although some accounts credit the Victoria with four-wheel brakes, in fact both cars had rear-wheel brakes only, rod operated on the Spanish car, cable on the Gwynne. The Victoria used either wire spoke or disc wheels as opposed to the Gwynne's artillery type. In overall dimensions the Gwynne is heavier at 585 kgs than the Victoria at some 400 kgs. This is so despite the fact that, whereas the tracks seem to be the same, the wheelbase of the Eight at 7ft 3in. is shorter than that of the Victoria at 7ft 9^1/$_2$ ins. Obviously the Eight's body is bigger and its transmission heavier but the extent of the difference is such as to suggest that the redesigned British version was rather more substantially built than its Spanish predecessor.

The Gwynne Eight chassis.

Although the Elizalde factory produced cars in Barcelona for a number of years, the Victoria was made by the Madrid firm of Talleres Franco-Espanoles. Dr Miguel told us that this came about when another of his brothers passed the design of the small car to the firm's agent who sold it to the Talleres without permission. When Arturo discovered this, he was so enraged that he dismissed the agent and disinherited his son to whom he was not reconciled until shortly before his death.

It has not been possible to discover either in this country or in Spain how and on what terms Mr Gwynne acquired the rights to manufacture the car. In a letter referred to in the May 1942 issue of *Motor Sport*, Mr Gwynne stated that the original Gwynne Eight was designed by a Frenchman in Spain. Obviously the Talleres led him to understand that the design was theirs to sell and their full name suggested a French connection. Dr Miguel, however, is adamant that no French element was involved. The only two French employees of the Elizalde concern had returned to France shortly after the outbreak of war.

Mr Gwynne went on to say that the car was in fact bought by

Gwynnes Engineering. Other sources in Spain, however, refer to the factory having been bought by Gwynnes. This must be regarded as highly unlikely given that they already had a fully-equipped works up and running for which they were seeking suitable work. The reference could perhaps be to the purchase of some jigs and tools in addition to drawings.

As ever in this story there is doubt about how many Victorias were made in the period of its manufacture from 1917 to 1921. Georgano puts the figure at '...about 1,000 in all'. The Spanish motor historian, J. Ciuro, however, gives these detailed figures:

Bore and Stroke	Engine Capacity	Production
55 mm x 100 mm	950 cc	40 to 50 Units
57 mm x 100 mm	1,020 cc	30 to 40 Units
59 mm x 100 mm	1,093 cc	2 Units
60 mm x 100 mm	1,130 cc	6 Units

plus one special sports car making at most 100 cars in all.

Even these figures are doubtful however. The surviving Victoria, which was made in 1917, has an engine number of 69. The more reliable chassis number is not known. Its owner was assisted in its restoration by two former employees of the Talleres. He estimated the total production at 300. Interestingly he included in that total "...the sales via the factory in England". Could it be that some early Gwynne Eights were in fact Victoria chassis clad in Gwynne or even Albert livery? We do know that Gwynne Eight chassis numbering started at 006.

Further clarification of the position has failed. What seems possible is that Georgano's figure of 1,000 Victorias includes commercial vehicles and buses made by the Talleres in its first period of manufacture and that the more likely figure for the Elizalde-designed 950 cc car was no more than 300.

The Gwynne Eight Itself

When it was first announced in October 1922, the Gwynne Eight, though well received by the motoring press as an attractive small car with lively performance, was already late to take advantage of the boom in popular motoring which followed the First World War

Moreover the main British manufacturers such as Austin, Rover, Singer and Wolseley were already re-established and, with newcomers like Morris and Ford were beginning to dominate the market.

The Gwynne Eight Motor Car.

The new car was powered by a four-cylinder pushrod-operated over-head valve engine of clean appearance which developed 24 bhp. The bore was 55 mm and the stroke 100 mm giving a capacity of 950 cc. The specification provided a three-bearing crankshaft, forced lubrication, aluminium alloy pistons and thermo-siphon cooling which, with an aluminium body, gave the car an excellent power to weight ratio. Transmission was by leather-lined inverted cone clutch coupled to a three-speed gearbox by flexible fabric couplings and a short splined shaft. The gearbox was mounted on the forward end of a torque tube and the torque was taken up by a ball-joint on the offside of the gearbox and a chassis cross-member. The gear ratios were 14.25:1, 9.2:1 and 4.83:1. Half-elliptic springs were fitted all round with the rear ones mounted on trunnions allowing the axle casing to rotate as much as the torque tube would allow.

There is some doubt about the type of final drive fitted. In its introductory article on the model on 20 October 1922, the *Light Car & Cyclecar* spoke of a spiral bevel whereas in its own road test report of the following January it referred specifically to a straight bevel as did

The Autocar on 18 May of that year. The authoritative *Automobile Engineer* of August 1923 was, however, quite clear that the crown wheel was by then of spiral cut.

The Treasury rating of 7.5 hp enabled the car to qualify for the lowest rate of Road Tax. It was offered at 198 guineas (£207 18s.) either with the clover-leaf body which became known as the hipbath or as a two-seater. The hipbath body had the advantage over the two-seater with dickey, in that all the occupants were under cover in the wet.

Accommodation was for two adults in the front and two children behind. A self-starter cost 10 guineas (£10 10s.) extra. A de luxe two-seater was available at 250 guineas (£262 10s.).

The Gwynne Eight 4-cylinder overhead valve engine. The car used a drip-feed petrol supply to an SU carburettor. Car featured XO-1866.

The standard two-seater Gwynne Eight body.

Altogether it was an attractive small car, advanced for its day and well received by the trade and technical journals. It was, moreover, one which was to form the basis of numerous specials over the years because its engine was capable of considerable development. Perhaps ominously, however, the Austin Seven made its appearance around the same time: its two-seater cost only £165.

The Gwynne Eight engine showing the self-starter at 10 guineas extra.

Distribution of the Eight was again in the hands of the Service Motor Co. Ltd, subsequently of 94 Great Portland Street, London, W1. Despite the car's appearance on Stand 314 at the 1922 Motor Show, the distributors felt it necessary to announce in the *Light Car & Cyclecar* of 5 January 1923 that:

> ...delivery will commence in the immediate future. At the present time a large number of these cars are undergoing strenuous and extensive road tests to ensure that every detail of their construction shall be thoroughly tried out before production models get into the hands of the public.

It could be that this time was used, following transmission problems with early Alberts, to change from the straight cut final drive used on models tested in the January to the spiral bevel used by April in the production models.

THE SERVICE MOTOR COMPANY Ltd.
TELEPHONE:
MAYFAIR 3025-6   94 GREAT PORTLAND STREET, LONDON. W.1.   TELEGRAMS:
                       AND 300 AGENTS THROUGHOUT THE COUNTRY.   SERAUTOGO. 'PHONE LONDON

THE GWYNNE EIGHT.
If you are interested in Motoring at an all-in cost comparable with 3rd class rail fare, get in touch with us for a demonstration.

Above & opposite: The Service Motor Company advertisement for the Gwynne Eight.
Reproduced by kind permission of the Hammersmith and Fulham Archives.

At the same time the magazine tested the car and introduced its report with the comment that it was not often that it was given the chance of taking over a car which had just returned from such a gruelling experience as the London–Exeter–London Trial since when it had had no tuning whatsoever. In that event C. Dickenson was one of only 69 finishers of 101 starters and won a Gold Medal. The report concluded that if the car was any better when it set out for Exeter than when it was handed over almost immediately after its return then it must have astonishing qualities for, without exaggeration, the testers found it to be one of the most lively and powerful small fours they had tested so far. Performance figures gave over 52 mph as a maximum and 46 mpg. A bright start indeed!

In February 1923 Gwynnes told trade journals that output was running at 100 cars each week and that between January and July several hundred cars were produced but some time later production was

BRIEF SPECIFICATION OF THE GWYNNE-EIGHT LIGHT CAR.

ENGINE	Four-cylinder Water Cooled.
	55 m.m. Bore × 100 m.m. Stroke
R.A.C. RATING	7'5
TAX	£8
RADIATOR	Honeycomb
COOLING	Thermo-syphon
CARBURETTOR	Automatic
LUBRICATION	Forced direct to all Main Bearings
IGNITION	H.T. Magneto
CLUTCH	Inverted Cone, Leather Faced
GEAR	Sliding Type, Gate Controlled, 3 Speeds and Reverse
RATIOS	1st, 14'25 to 1 ; 2nd, 9'2 to 1 ; Top, 4'83 to 1 ; Reverse, 14'25 to 1
FINAL DRIVE	Straight Bevel
TRANSMISSION	Enclosed Propellor Shaft
STEERING	Worm and Complete Worm Wheel
WHEELS	Dunlop Steel Detachable, 700 × 80 m.m.
REAR AXLE	Semi-floating
WHEEL BASE	7 feet 3 inches
TRACK	3 feet 6 inches

MODELS.

2/3 seater Utility or 2 seater Body   198 Guineas

Each well Upholstered, with Hood, Screen, Three Lamps, C.A.V. Lighting Set with Dynamo. Five Detachable Wheels and Tyres, Kit of Tools, etc.

ELECTRIC SELF-STARTER............   **10 Guineas Extra**

2 seater De Luxe with Dickey seat.   250 Guineas

Upholstered in Real Leather, with Double Windscreen, Electric Starter, Dynamo Lighting (C.A.V.), Five Detachable Wheels and Tyres, Kit of Tools, Clock, Speedometer and Service All-Weather Equipment.

Costing but little more than a Motor Cycle and Sidecar Combination, yet infinitely superior in respect of every desirable quality, the "GWYNNE EIGHT" is a First-Class "Real" Motor Car on a small scale. With over 40 miles per gallon as the average petrol consumption, and an attainable speed of over 50 miles per hour, the "GWYNNE-EIGHT" will compete with many cars of double its horse-power at half the running costs.

We shall be happy to arrange a trial run at any time at your convenience and without any further obligation on your part.

There is no better value at the price!

brought to a halt by the first of what was to prove to be Gwynne's several financial problems. By July a Receiver and Manager had been appointed to Gwynnes Engineering and he stopped production while he considered the financial situation.

The following October the trade press carried the announcement that: 'The famous Gwynne 8 and 14 are once more in full production. Happily the little problems of production have been solved...'. This was obviously 'tradespeak' for the fact that the Receiver had made arrangements to finance production once more. Unfortunately though, under the rules of the Society of Motor Manufacturers and Traders, Gwynnes could not exhibit at the 1923 Motor Show whilst in Receivership.

A full four-seater had been introduced in May 1923. This had a split front seat to allow easier access to the rear seats. Initially, however, it was not a newly designed body but rather an extended hipbath with an extra rear section welded on which meant that the back seat passengers sat outside the existing wheelbase. At the same time a fully-framed windscreen replaced the original half-frame. This enabled the hood to be fixed firmly and the upper part of the screen to be opened to make it easier to drive in the rain.

March 1924 saw further improvements such as the provision of a wider door, better weather equipment and the elimination of the rear footwells to increase passenger comfort. A self-starter and a speedometer were now no longer treated as extras. The prices for 1924 were originally announced as £180 for the chassis, the two-seater was £210 or £255 as a de luxe, the hipbath £215 and a full four-seater de luxe was £260. By March the four-seater was marketed at £235 and was advertised as achieving 55 to 60 mph and 45 to 50 mpg. The reduction in price may have had something to do with the fact that this was the time when Gwynnes dispensed with their sole concessionaires The Service Motor Co. and took on sales and distribution themselves.

Undoubtedly, savings in costs were the main motivation for this action though it might also have been considered that Mr Mitcheson was over-reaching himself as he had opened several other enterprises. These included a finance house at 95 Great Portland Street and the Portland Equipment Company at No. 80. This last was primarily to push the successful Gwynne patent All-Weather Head. Moreover, Mr Mitcheson was actively fostering his candidature for a Parliamentary seat at Bradford in Yorkshire.

"On a 'Gwynne Eight' you'll never be late."

What the experts say: "On a Gwynne Eight you'll never be late."

However, there was a price to be paid. Mr Mitcheson had success-fully kept Gwynne's products in the public eye by his active advertis-ing campaign but, perhaps even more importantly he had provided them with a West End showroom in what was then the very centre of the motor-car trade, Great Portland Street.

Production at this point was said to be 50 cars per week. About this time, too, the Receiver further rationalised production by reducing the range of Eights to two models, the four-seater tourer and the two-seater sports. The Fourteen range was also reduced to tourer and All-Weather. The cars were still available in chassis form at £180 and £360.

The sports model was an attractive, polished aluminium two-seater with pointed tail and nickel-plated radiator shell first announced in April 1924. It was priced at £275. Its introduction may have been due to the sporting interests of Mr J. F. Deverill who had joined Gwynnes from the Service organisation to take responsibility for sales. With David Chinery, the main London agent, he became the company's most successful competition driver. Another factor may have been the introduction by Chinery of his own 'Olympia' sports Eight with tuned engine at £275. This was guaranteed to achieve 70 mph after it had been run in for 500 miles. Chinery claimed that no other car capable of such a guaranteed speed was available at under £450.

The Gwynne Eight 'Brooklands' model owned by D. L. Vinall, Adelaide, South Australia.

By early 1925, Gwynne's own sports car had been developed into the well-known Brooklands model. Differences from the standard car

included larger valves and stronger valve springs, larger bore carburettor and wider diameter induction pipe, a high lift cam and higher
ratio back axle. The accelerator pedal was no longer central but had
been moved to the offside. The car was guaranteed to achieve 65 mph
– no mean achievement for a small car of that era.

*The Gwynne
Eight 1925
'Brooklands'
owned by D.
K. Woodburn,
England,
shown here in
competition
in the Light
Car section
of the VSCC
1998 Welsh
Trial.*

In April 1925, the price of the four-seater was reduced to £190. No
doubt this was to try to compete with the four-seater Austin Seven
which by then was available at £149. The following month Mr
Gwynne purchased the car side of Gwynnes Engineering from the
Receiver and formed Gwynne Cars, Ltd. Clearly this prompted a
fundamental review of the product and its market which, it would
seem, concluded that the existing standard four-seater no longer met
the needs of the family man. Despite its proven sporting performance
in numerous trials, hill-climbs and races, it was too cramped and comparatively unrefined to flourish as a family vehicle. It was accordingly
decided to redesign the car. It was to reappear as the 'R' type.

Widespread and exhaustive search of public archives and private
sources has failed to establish exactly how many Eights were manufactured. The best estimate from correlation of known facts such as
chassis and engine numbers and dates of first registration, periods of
production and known non-production, etc., is that, at most, 2,250 cars
of the original type were made. As to survivors, there are fourteen

Eight cars on the UK Register. Of these six are in roadworthy condition, four are under active restoration and one is in a museum.

The Gwynne Eight with the R.E.A.L. body. This body was made by the R.E.A.L. Body Company of Chiswick, the company having been founded by R. E. Alman. They subsequently moved to Ealing and produced bodies for many other manufacturers.

In Australia, where Gwynnes had a thriving export trade, there are nine known survivors of which four are roadworthy. Two await rebuilding and one is in the process of being reimported from Australia. In addition there is one Eight (though it bears a Ten radiator) in a museum in New Zealand. This is an interesting car in that it was fitted with the proprietary Robertson variable automatic friction drive in this country in 1924 and between then and 1930 covered some 100,000 miles so equipped. It was still in this country in 1959 but was acquired by the museum around 1973.

All told, therefore, there are 23 known surviving Gwynne Eight cars. Fire appliances constructed on Gwynne Eight chassis are looked at seperately in Chapter Seven.

114

The 'R' Type Eight

The Eight was reintroduced as the 'R' Type in June 1926. The wheel-base was extended from 7ft 3in. to 7ft 9in., the track widened by 4in. to 3ft 10in. and longer and more substantial semi-elliptic front springs were fitted. This enlargement enabled a full-sized comfortable four-seater body to be fitted with rigid side-screens to provide better weather-proofing. A rear luggage rack housed the spare wheel so that two doors could be provided on the nearside as well as, for the first time, a driver's door. Headlamps were taken from their shaky place on the mudguards where they were replaced by side lights. The head-lamps themselves were mounted on brackets affixed to the front dumb irons. Low pressure tyres and front wheel brakes were optional extras and, again for the first time, an attractive four-door saloon was offered. In short, the Gwynne Eight had grown up. More to the point, the firm had decided that it should offer a family car and not a performance car.

The Gwynne Eight. Thought to be a photograph of the four seater 'R' Type Eight introduced in June 1926, or of a Gwynne Ten. There is some confusion due to the small number of 'R' Types made and the lack of surviving examples.

To deal with all the extra weight, the bore of the engine was increased from 53 mm to 55 mm (1,020 cc). A more robust centre bearing was provided together with stronger valve springs but the overall design of the successful engine remained unchanged. The car not only looked a more substantial vehicle but, on test, it was described as quiet, comfortable, free from vibration, sturdy and incorporating sound engineering practices.

The 'R' Eight sold at £250 for the two-seater and the standard four-seater. The sports model was continued at £285 and the price of the new saloon was set at £350. Equipment was complete, the only extra being front wheel brakes at £10.

No separate production figures exist for the model but as there are no known survivors, the output must have been small. There are believed to be some parts of an 'R' type in Northern Ireland but nothing more is known about these and they are not believed to be substantial enough to enable a car to be restored.

Re-introduction of the Eight

In October 1927 the firm re-introduced the Eight which had been dropped in favour of the wholly-new Ten. This was in the form of a fabric or panelled sports car using the 'R' type engine of 1020 cc. It was known as the 8/24 model.

The usual Gwynne features of leather-cone clutch, three-speed gearbox on the front end of the torque tube and enclosed propeller shaft to a spiral bevel rear axle were retained. Ignition, as ever, was by magneto but brakes were now on all four wheels. Gear ratios at 4.83:1, 8.2:1 and 14.25:1 differed from those of the standard 'R' type which were 5.1:1, 8.65:1 and 15.0:1.

The fact that the car was contemporaneous with the newly-designed Ten yet continued to use the features of a withdrawn model suggests that the company was prudently using up surplus stocks of parts. Even so the motoring press concluded that an 80 mph sports car at £265 was, while not cheap, good value. A hood could be provided to special order! No production numbers or survivors are known.

The Gwynne Ten

The Ten was introduced in March 1927 to replace the Eight which, even with its uprated specification, was proving to be uncompetitive both in price and performance.

The Ten incorporated a number of substantial technical changes not least of which was the departure from Gwynne's traditional feature of the cross-flow cylinder head. The main changes included increasing the bore from 57 mm to 63 mm and thereby the capacity from 1,020 cc to 1,247 cc and the Treasury rating from 8 hp to 10 hp. At the same time the brake horse power was raised from 24 to 30. The inlet and exhaust manifolds were combined on the nearside with the exhaust discharging from the front of the engine and not as before. The rockers became forced lubricated, a Solex carburettor replaced the SU and coil ignition replaced the magneto. A dynamotor was placed off-side at the front of the cylinder block. The crankcase was of cast iron.

The chassis was lengthened to provide an 8ft. wheelbase and four wheel brakes were fitted as standard at last.

A number of familiar Gwynne features remained, however. These included a three-bearing crankshaft, pushrod-operated valves, transmission via a cone clutch to a three-speed gearbox and thence through flexible disc coupling and enclosed propeller shaft to a spiral bevel rear axle. Cooling was, as ever, by thermo-siphon and fuel supply by gravity feed from a tank below the scuttle. The gear ratios were 5.0:1, 8.65:1 and 15.0:1.

On the road 60 mph was guaranteed though over 70 mph was achievable with fuel consumption at an average of 40 mpg. Once again the car's outstanding ability to amble along at around 5 mph in top gear and then to accelerate smoothly without changing gear to over 50 mph was remarked upon.

The Gwynne Ten. Car shown is owned by J. Warburton.

Responsibility for sales of the Ten was taken on by Sidney G. Cummings of Fulham, the well-known racing and trials driver of the 1920s. Despite an enthusiastic sales campaign throughout 1927 and 1928 (in marked contrast to the virtual absence of publicity since the marque's heyday from 1923 to 1925) the initiative was not commercially successful. Low volume production and the lack of a nationwide service organisation simply would not allow Gwynnes to compete with the major league players.

The car was available in a number of styles. Apart from the standard tourer at £225 and an open two-seater at £220, there were five saloon variants and two sports cars at £230 and £260 respectively. The saloons comprised a standard steel model at £285; a fabric job at the same price or, on the sports chassis at £315. Finally, a Gordon England saloon was advertised for £265 or, on the sports chassis, at £295. Such a proliferation of models in so limited a volume could hardly have been an efficient means of production. Indeed, Gwynnes themselves stressed in advertising that their cars were not mass-produced but were hand-finished.

Although the Ten probably ceased to be produced late in 1929, the cars were still advertised by Cummings in March 1930. It is not now clear whether these were from unsold stock or whether some few cars were being nailed together in the factory which did not close its doors until 7 December 1930 when the works manager was paid off. Some wages continued to be paid, presumably to office staff involved in the winding-up, until as late as 29 May 1931.

Any estimate of the number of Gwynne Tens made must necessarily be based upon the flimsiest evidence because only one surviving car (recently re-imported from Australia) is known, though there are persistent rumours of a second in the Melbourne area of Australia. The chassis number of the surviving Ten is 212 in a series which is known to have started at 200. A spare engine supplied with the car also bears the low number of 210. Both figures suggest a minimal output.

However, in a letter dated 27 December 1927 from Gwynne Cars, Ltd to its main agent in Northern Ireland, the firm referred to having arranged finance for the manufacture of 300 cars in 1928 – yet further confirmation of its chronic under-capitalisation. The only press indication of production numbers that have been seen is in *The Automotor Journal* of 15 March 1928 when, in his road test report, the writer commented that the output for the following five weeks was already booked but that, after that, Mr Cummings hoped to get about twenty chassis each week from the works. This was clearly exaggerated sales talk given the overall limit of 300 cars for the year yet it does suggest a regular, though limited, flow of cars. A few of the 300 would have been of the revised 14/40 model and, perhaps, of the 8/24 yet most would have been Tens. If the same conditions of financial stringency applied throughout the Ten's life, then it is doubtful whether as many as 500 were made over the two years and nine months of the car's known production life. Indeed, it could well have been far less despite the publicity photographs which showed at least six different body styles available. One other indication which supports so small a total was contained in the article of July 1965 to which I have already referred. This quoted C. M. C. Turner as recalling that, by 1927, the firm was building "...only a handful of cars a week...". This could well be interpreted as five or six which would be consonant with 300 per annum.

In these circumstances one is bound to ask how, on technical or financial grounds, the management of the company could justify the costly redesign of both its larger and smaller models when it had to go cap in hand to the bank to borrow the money for each year's production. No doubt more of Mr Gwynne's personal fortune was lost in the vain hope of continuing to help the marque survive.

Gwynnes in Competition

From the outset, Gwynnes realised the value in sales terms of success in competition and took part enthusiastically. They had some success with the later Albert models but it was not until the introduction of the Gwynne Eight that the concern really began to shine. Not only did they enter such events as hill climbs and reliability trials organised by local motor clubs, but, more to the point, were their successes in national events such as those for which the Royal Automobile Club (RAC), the Junior Car Club (JCC) and the Auto-Cycle Union (ACU) were responsible.

In 1924 Gwynnes advertised the fact that the Eight had won over 90 First Class awards in the previous year. It was in 1924, too, that the Eight won its most prestigious awards. It was joint first in the premier award of the Westall Cup for the JCC's Efficiency Trial and first in the RAC's Six Day Trial. In both cases the driver was David Chinery, the main London agent and the Gwynne's most successful competition driver. Close behind him was J. F. Deverill who had been responsible for Albert and Gwynne sales when the Service Motor Company was the sole concessionaire and who moved to Gwynnes in March 1924 when the company took over its own sales and distribution.

Apart from the Gold Medals awarded to Chinery, C. M. C. Turner and A. H. Bartley in high speed reliability events run by the JCC, little activity was shown in competition by Gwynnes in 1925 when, of course, the purchase of the car business from the Receiver was being negotiated by Nevile Gwynne.

The most notable event in 1926 was Turner's participation in the JCC 200-mile race at Brooklands. For this event, to use his own words, he:

...financed Gwynnes to build him a proper racer. The side members of an Eight were modified to pass beneath the back axle, which was sprung on Gwynne 14 front springs adapted as cantilevers, while the axle casing was cast in light alloy. Laystall provided a special camshaft and a crankshaft with cased-in bob-weights on the webs and the block was bored out from 55 mm to 60 mm giving a capacity of 1,087 cc. Carburation was by twin SUs...and a huge fuel tank formed the undershield of the car, petrol feed being by hand pump supplemented by a wind-driven pump outrigged above the tail. The three-speed gearbox was retained. A very fine fabric streamlined body was built for the car by Gordon England and the radiator and dumb-irons were cowled in by alloy sheeting. A modified Rover front axle fitted with Whitehead brakes having special ribbed drums provided retardation suitable for the 'road' circuit the J.C.C. had devised... The compression was raised to around 10:1 and the fuel changed from petrol to Discol... The Gwynne was then capable of 92 mph.

The car finished 6th out of 7 in its class from 15 starters and 12th overall at an average of 58.91 mph.

For the 1927 version of the event, Turner grew more ambitious. The fuel was changed again, this time to the new ethyl-leaded type. This proved too much. The six studs securing the cylinder block broke, the carburettors spilled fuel under vibration and the car caught fire. The chassis was saved and sold. It was last heard of in the 1950s when it formed the basis of a sports 'special'. No more is known about it other than that it had a radiator taken from a Singer and that it bore the registration number MP-5645.

The last year in which there was active participation in competitions while Gwynnes were in production is an isolated example in 1928. By then even Chinery had deserted the marque in favour of Rileys. In that year, however, G. C. Strachan, the organising secretary of the Royal Ulster Automobile Club, entered his 'R' type Eight in the RAC Tourist Trophy race. He retired after two hours with a slipping clutch. The eventual winner was Kaye Don on a Lea-Francis.

David Woodburn racing at Silverstone in April 1960 in his 1925 Gwynne Eight Brooklands.

Little more was heard of Gwynnes in the competition sphere until after the Second World War when, attracted by the performance and longevity of the sturdy little Eights, several amateur drivers started to use them in the 1960s and 70s for race, trial and hill-climb events organised by the Vintage Sports Car Club. Prominent among them were John Missen, Ian Smith, Ian Walker and David Woodburn. The cars were still going strong at the end of the century by which time they, though not their drivers, were nearly 80 years old. An active Register keeps track of all the surviving cars at home and overseas and a quarterly newsletter amusingly entitled *The Gwynneformation Circular* keeps owners abreast of events, developments, cars for sale, spares availability and so on. Items of historical interest are also included.

(Above) Clare Woodburn driving at the VSCC 1998 Welsh Trial in a Gwynne Eight 'Montrosity'. The car was so named as it was owned by Montrose Motors in Alperton. This example was built in the 1970s.

Mechanically standard except for the 1925 gearbox.

(Left)
A Gwynne Ten in competition.

Chapter Seven

The Fire Appliances

GWYNNES REALISED early that the combination of their two main products, cars and pumps, lent itself to the manufacture of fire appliances. The first fire engine was introduced in October 1924 and was designed specifically for use in small country towns, on large estates or to supplement larger appliances in municipal fleets. It was based on the Gwynne Eight chassis. A larger engine was to follow and, eventually, the firm supplied pumps to be used with appliances manufactured by other contemporary firms of commercial vehicles. This chapter covers the full range of fire appliances with which the firm was concerned.

The Gwynne Eight Fire Engine
The chassis on which this fire engine is based is that of the standard Gwynne Eight car supplemented by two extra cross members aft of the rear axle to take the weight of the pump; extra leaves are fitted to the rear springs and the tyres are filled with Rubberine to avoid punctures.

The engine, too, is the same as that fitted to the car save that, in addition to the normal thermo-siphon cooling, a special connection from the fire pump into the rear of the cylinder block enables a flow of cold water to be maintained through the engine while the machine is stationary with the pump working.

A picture of the Fire Appliance from the sales brochure.
Photograph reproduced by kind permission of the Marconi Company Ltd.

The pump itself is of the two-stage turbine type with impellers arranged back to back to minimise end thrust. Facing the rear of the machine there is a central suction port of 3 in. diameter with a $2^1/2$ in. discharge port on each side of it. The pump provides 100 gallons of water per minute pumped against a pressure of 100 psi when running at 3,000 rpm giving an effective stream of some 80 feet. It will also supply two jets with 140 gallons per minute at 60 psi pressure.

The drive for the pump is via a transfer box on the engine side of the gearbox. This drive is transmitted via a dog clutch and a separate pro-peller shaft which lies above the vehicle shaft and is linked direct to the fire pump. The transfer box increases the engine speed one and a half fold to 3,000 rpm at the pump spindle. The drive is engaged by a lever protruding through the floor and a pair of interlocks ensure that the pump drive cannot be accidentally brought into operation while the vehicle is in motion. Nor can the vehicle be put into gear while the pump is working.

A centrifugal pump can produce little suction from the water source until it is primed. This is done by means of a built-in vacuum pump driven from the main pump spindle and linked to the centrifugal volute

The pump drive engage handle and the interlocks to prevent operation whilst the appliance is in motion.

through an interceptor tank. The vacuum pump is driven through friction rollers and serves to prime the main pump by drawing air from its interceptor tank. A pipe connects the bottom of the tank to the main pump through a stop valve. To prime the main pump the vacuum pump is clutched in and, when the interceptor tank is full, a ball float valve prevents water from entering the vacuum pump. The interceptor tank can then be drained into the main pump and in this way priming can be achieved.

The body of the appliance is designed with seating for the driver and one fireman. A handrail and wide running boards allow two more firemen to travel standing. Behind the driver's seat a partitioned box accommodates delivery hose, nozzle pipes and nozzles while two lengths of suction hose are strapped to its rear. In this form it would reach a speed of 45 mph with a full crew aboard. The author, in fact, drove one of the surviving engines and can vouch for its lively performance well over 70 years after it was manufactured.

This picture shows the wide running boards, the hoses and storage on the Gwynne Fire Appliance. Photograph reproduced by kind permission of the Marconi Company Ltd.

In their advertising literature Gwynnes made the point that the appliance is well adapted for such agricultural uses as spraying, irrigation and drainage, all functions for which the company had many years of experience at home and overseas. In such uses the pump, operating against a comparatively low head, could discharge a greater amount of water than when used for fire fighting.

The appliance cost £410 fully equipped at the time when the standard Gwynne Eight hipbath tourer cost £190.

We have little information about the total number of appliances made on the Eight chassis. In the issue of the *Commercial Motor* dated 18 September 1928, Gwynnes claimed to have sold:

...more than two dozen sets of both the self-propelled and trailer types mainly for use abroad. No fewer than fourteen sets have been exported to Japan (a Japanese translation of the instruction manual has been seen) and others to Spain, India and the Malay Straits.

It is thought that about eight were sold in this country of which two survive.

The better known of these is XU-9993, now owned by Marconi Communications, Ltd of New Century Park, Coventry, CV3 1HJ. Although said to have been built in 1922, this was first registered on 27 October 1924. For some years it was the factory demonstrator and, as such, was hired periodically by Selfridges, Ltd to hose down the exterior of their Oxford Street store in London. After Gwynnes motor car business was liquidated in 1929, Selfridges must have acquired it because, in 1939, it was bought from them by the Margaretting Parish Council in Essex through public subscription and restored by the local engineering firm. Because the Council was refused permission to use it operationally, they sold it on to GEC – Marconi, Ltd of Chelmsford where it gave yeoman service when the factory was subjected to an incendiary attack. Since then it went into honourable retirement while making regular appearances at local country fairs and so on. At the dismemberment of the GEC group of companies, the appliance was moved to Coventry where it is once again well cared for by the successor, Marconi Communications, Ltd.

The Gwynne Eight Fire Appliance. This example is owned and maintained by Marconi.
Photograph reproduced by kind permission of the Marconi Company Ltd.

The other appliance – PW-6679 – was first registered on 4 December 1925 and is believed to have been in service with the Norfolk County Fire Brigade at Downham Market from new until it was decommissioned around 1960. It was later acquired and restored by the late Dick Joice then of East Dereham. The appliance now rests in the Byegones Museum at Holkham Hall, Norfolk.

A third appliance – NU-360 – is, in fact, a replica constructed on the chassis of a hipbath G8 by C. H. (Bill) Peacock, the President of the Gwynne Register. It was first registered as a standard hipbath tourer on 11 April 1923 and, after passing through several hands, was found, rebuilt and sold by him at a Beaulieu auction in July 1962. It is now owned by a Somerset enthusiast. This is a perfect example of how easily a false provenance can be established. A previous owner told the author that the appliance had originally been supplied to a royal estate on the Isle of Wight but that he had bought it from the owner of a manor house in Gwent!

Gwynne Fourteen Fire Engine

A larger appliance based on the Gwynne Fourteen engine of 1,944 cc was also offered at £775 fully equipped at a time when, in 1928, the

127

tourer cost £285. The pump in this case provided 250 gallons per minute at 135 psi ranging to 400 gallons at 70 psi. No information about how many of these units were made, where they were used or whether any have survived has been discovered. There does exist, however, a photograph of a 250 gallon trailer pump fitted with Spencer-Moulton solid tyres in the livery of the Secunderabad Cantonment Authority in India. The same livery (and tyres) are borne by the engine in the photograph and so there is a presumption (no more) that it, too, was exported to India.

Gwynne Trailer Pumps

In addition to the self-propelled appliances described above which were powered by G8 and G14 engines, Gwynnes offered trailer pumps of 100 gallon and 250 gallon capacity similarly powered. These were advertised as being suitable for hand-towing or for trailing behind any vehicle. The fact that they could be easily manoeuvred by hand made them particularly suitable for businesses based on a cluster of small buildings. The 100 gallon version cost £258 at the factory or £267 F.O.B. London for export.

The Gwynne Eight Fire Appliance and Trailer Pump.

Research over several years has revealed no trace of surviving trailer pumps powered by Gwynne engines. However, an advertisement in the August 1989 edition of the magazine *Practical Classics* alerted us to yet another aspect of Gwynne's fire-fighting activities. This offered for sale a small trailer pump the radiator of which bore the name 'Standard' while the pump had 'Standard-Gwynne' cast into its body. These small pumps were used extensively in the Second World War by the Auxiliary Fire Service and were normally towed behind Bedford vans. Originally Gwynnes, by then long owned by Wm

(Opposite & below) Front & rear views of the Gwynne Fourteen Fire Appliance. This example showing solid tyres and the Gwynne Invincible badge can be seen on the side of the unit.
Photographs reproduced by kind permission of the Marconi Company Ltd.

Foster & Co. of Lincoln, provided the pumps, which had single stage conventional impellers, with Standard Eight engines as prime movers though sometimes Coventry Climax engines were used. Eventually the whole unit was made under licence by Standard Motors, Ltd of Coventry.

In all some 6,000 such trailer pumps were made, a number of which are known by the Fire Service Preservation Society to survive.

Gwynne Pumps in Other Makes of Vehicle

Although Gwynnes ceased to make vehicles around 1929, Gwynne pumps continued to be manufactured, first as a subsidiary of Wm Foster & Co. of Lincoln from 1927 and, later, as a subsidiary of W. H. Allen of Bedford. They thus remained available to other makers of fire-fighting equipment. Most notably this was in conjunction with Morris Commercial, Ltd of Foundry Lane, Soho, Birmingham, who produced a series of Morris-Gwynne appliances. The earliest announcement traced was in September 1926 of an engine carrying ten to twelve men and a 30 foot ladder. This was based on a standard 25/ 30 cwt chassis with a four-cylinder 15.9 hp engine capable of a road speed of 40 mph. The price was £765 ex-works.

The Morris-Commercial Ltd Fire Appliance.

Unhappily very little information by way of Morris Commercial production records has survived and that which has relates only to vehicle types and not to the uses to which they were put. Virtually all that is known, therefore, is culled from announcements of purchases by individual fire authorities in trade magazines such as *Commercial Motor* or from a surviving Gwynne sales catalogue of 1931. Dartford, Kent, for example, had a fleet of five of the one-ton Morris Commercials. Others appeared on the TX chassis in the liveries of Flint, Canterbury, Chesham and some Scottish authorities. Bridport in Dorset bought an appliance on the six-wheeler chassis.

The six-wheeler fire appliance made by Morris Commercial Cars Ltd.

One on the TX chassis which has survived is OV-9730 which is owned and was restored by Nick Baldwin, the motoring historian. This was first registered in May 1932. It is in the livery of the GEC Witton works and was last taxed by that company in 1964. It was found, ironically, standing in two feet of water in the basement of a Birmingham garage.

Fire Float

Finally, in a brochure issued in 1927 by Gwynne Pumps, Ltd as a Foster subsidiary, the company reported having supplied some one hundred pumps to Fire Brigades at home and overseas. Of these, the former London County Council had forty, thirty eight of which were in fire engines and two on the fire float 'Gamma II'. The latter delivered through eight jets at 1,200 gallons per minute at a pressure of 120 psi or alternatively 1,600 gallons at 90 psi.

Yet another example of the diversity of Gwynne products.

Coda

Though now remote from Gwynnes themselves, it may be of interest to record briefly the present situation at the sites where Gwynne products were made.

As to the London area premises occupied by the Gwynne family concerns themselves, the original works off the Strand are readily recognisable down the steps at the bottom of Essex Street. They now form part of the Temple Library. The Brooke Street works, however, long ago disappeared as the High Holborn headquarters of the Prudential Assurance Co. expanded. At that time the firm's foundry was in Parker Street off Holborn Kingsway but that area, too, is now entirely occupied by modern office blocks.

The first premises recorded in the Hammersmith rate books as occupied by Gwynnes were surprisingly ascribed to George and Henry rather than John Gwynne. This must have been the George who later went to Australia. The premises comprised: 'Iron works, steam machinery (part finished) and land at Riverside House'. By 1872, George and Henry also owned houses at No. 8 to 12 Queens Road and occupied a room over the gateway together with a workshop in Chancellor Street all on the other side of the road from the main works. Queens Road has been renamed Crisp Road and the houses have now been replaced by large blocks of municipal flats. The workshop in Chancellor Street is still readily identifiable though it has been adapted as living accommodation. The main pump works, with the addition of a modern foyer and a few licks of paint, have now become the BBC Riverside Studios after having passed through the hands of one or two film companies.

In 1931, several years after Gwynnes moved to Lincoln as part of William Foster & Co. Ltd, a costing and estimating office was built at the corner of Crisp and Chancellor Roads. That still stands. The firm's name, which was incised over the main entrance, has been obliterated and, with the addition of a new mansard roof housing more rooms, the building is currently occupied by JAC Travel, Ltd.

The costing and estimating office as it stands today.

The aeroplane engine and motor car works on Church Wharf at the end of Chiswick Mall remained empty for many years after Gwynne Cars, Ltd finally closed the gates in 1931. It is now the site of some modern town houses and a light industrial estate. We have recently been made aware that, when he made a painting of Chiswick Eyot, Lucien Pissarro, son of the famous French Impressionist, included the end elevation of this factory and, unusually for an impressionist painter, he quite clearly outlined part of the name 'Gwynnes Engineering'. Fame indeed! In addition, a local road in the area has recently been named 'Gwynne Close'.

Ealing Park Foundry was situated on Junction Road, London, W5. This road runs parallel to the main Windmill Road in Little Ealing. The foundry continued to operate until 1964 (latterly for Qualcast, Ltd). It was later replaced, to the great relief of the neighbouring house-holders, by a small block of flats. During its existence there had been several court cases in which complaints had been heard about noise and nuisance.

The Albert motor works in Glasshouse Street (now Mall) off the Albert Embankment, Vauxhall, London, SE11, is still recognisably a small factory site. Part is occupied by BMW Ltd and part by a firm of fine art shippers called Martinspeed, Ltd. After Gwynnes took over from Adam, Grimaldi, Ltd, the makers of the Albert car, the cramped premises became their body works.

The old Albert Motor Works as pictured today.

The only other known Gwynnes site was that of Lang Propellers, Ltd originally of Weybridge, Surrey. By 1916 the firm was forced by the huge wartime demand for its product to seek larger premises and this it found in Hamm Moor Lane, Addlestone, Surrey. The firm was presumably purchased by Gwynnes for its timber quota and its manufacturing capacity which was needed to expand car body production. Langs closed in 1922 and was formally liquidated around May 1924. The main works buildings survived until recently in the hands of Peabody Foods but the area is now being redeveloped for housing.

There is also an Albert Wharf in Gwynne Road, Battersea, London, SW11 but that that relates to the personal land holdings of James Eglington Anderson Gwynne and not to the Gwynne commercial and industrial activities.

And so, in this age of rationalisation, amalgamation and take-over, the name Gwynne along with those of so many erstwhile British manufacturing companies, has passed into industrial history. Ironically it is today kept alive mainly by the forty or so surviving examples of the very product which undermined its prosperity in the first place – the Gwynne motor car.

The Gwynne Motor Car Company plaque